The Spiritual Body:
A Devotional Journey Through 1 Corinthians 12–16

Exploring Spiritual Gifts, Love, and the Hope of Resurrection

BROOKE HOLT

The Spiritual Body:
A Devotional Journey Through 1 Corinthians 12-16
Exploring Spiritual Gifts, Love, and the Hope of Resurrection

©2025 Brooke Holt. All rights reserved.

"Now you are the body of Christ and individually members of it."
– 1 Corinthians 12:27

Published in Jacksonville, Florida by Bible Study Media, Inc.

ISBN # 978-1-942243-70-0

Ebook ISBN # 978-1-942243-71-7

No part of this publication may be reproduced, stored in a retrieval system, or transmitted in any form or by any means electronic, mechanical, photocopy, recording, or otherwise, except for brief quotations in printed reviews without the publisher's prior written permission. www.biblestudymedia.com.

Unless otherwise indicated, all Scripture quotations are from the ESV® Bible (The Holy Bible, English Standard Version®), copyright © 2001 by Crossway, a publishing ministry of Good News Publishers. Used by permission. All rights reserved.

Bible Study Media, Inc.
Igniting Hearts. Engaging Minds.

Printed in the United States of America.

Table *of* Contents

An Epiphany Journey: From Glory to Glory — 6

Introduction: The Spiritual Body — 8

Week 1: The Spiritual Gifts in the Body of Christ

Day 1: A Spiritual Reorientation and Test — 12
1 Corinthians 12:1-3

Day 2: God Desires to Empower You for the Common Good — 14
1 Corinthians 12:4-7

Day 3: God's Prerogative in the Giving of Gifts — 16
1 Corinthians 12:8-11

Day 4: Unity and Equality in the Body of Christ — 18
1 Corinthians 12:12-13

Day 5: Breaking the Bondage of Pride and Insecurity — 20
1 Corinthians 12:14-18

Day 6: One Body of Christ — 22
1 Corinthians 12:19-26

Day 7: Do You Desire the Higher Gifts? — 24
1 Corinthians 12:27-31

Week 2: Love, the More Excellent Way

Day 8: Spiritual Gifts Require Spiritual Maturity — 28
1 Corinthians 13:1-3

Day 9: The Full Expression of Love — 30
1 Corinthians 13:4-7

Day 10: An Eternal Focus — 32
1 Corinthians 13:8-10

Day 11: The Most Excellent Way — 34
1 Corinthians 13:11-13

Day 12: Do You Need Some Spiritual Redirection? — 36
1 Corinthians 14:1-5

Day 13: The Body of Christ Is Meant to Live in Harmony — 38
1 Corinthians 14:6-8

Day 14: Are You Speaking in a Foreign Language? — 40
1 Corinthians 14:9-12

Week 3: Building Up the Body in Love

Day 15:	Private Versus Corporate Expressions of Prayer and Praise *1 Corinthians 14:13-15*	44
Day 16:	It Is Not About You! *1 Corinthians 14:16-17*	46
Day 17:	Two Extreme Views of the Spiritual Gifts *1 Corinthians 14:18-19*	48
Day 18:	Grow Up in the Lord! *1 Corinthians 14:20-22*	50
Day 19:	The Faithful Practice of Spiritual Gifts *1 Corinthians 14:23-25*	52
Day 20:	Order Leads to Edification *1 Corinthians 14:26-32*	54
Day 21:	Order and Peace in the Church *1 Corinthians 14:33-35*	56

Week 4: The Hope of the Resurrection

Day 22:	People Under Authority *1 Corinthians 14:36-40*	60
Day 23:	Are You Being Saved by the Gospel? *1 Corinthians 15:1-2*	62
Day 24:	The Things of First Importance *1 Corinthians 15:3-8*	64
Day 25:	The Transformative Grace of God *1 Corinthians 15:9-11*	66
Day 26:	Is Your Faith in Vain? *1 Corinthians 15:12-15*	68
Day 27:	The People Who Are to Be Most Pitied *1 Corinthians 15:16-19*	70
Day 28:	The Victory of Jesus! *1 Corinthians 15:20-25*	72

Week 5: The Glory of the Resurrection

Day 29:	Godly Humility and Hope *1 Corinthians 15:26-28*	76
Day 30:	How Do We Live in the Now but Not Yet? *1 Corinthians 15:29-34*	78
Day 31:	The Hope of a Resurrected Body *1 Corinthians 15:35-38*	80
Day 32:	A Future Glory for You *1 Corinthians 15:39-41*	82
Day 33:	The Glory That Awaits You *1 Corinthians 15:42-44*	84
Day 34:	A Mystery Revealed *1 Corinthians 15:45-53*	86
Day 35:	You Have Victory Through Jesus Christ *1 Corinthians 15:54-58*	88

Week 6: Living as the Body of Christ

Day 36:	The Lord's Day *1 Corinthians 16:1-4*	92
Day 37:	Is There Adversity in Fruitful Ministry? *1 Corinthians 16:5-8*	94
Day 38:	Let All That You Do Be Done in Love *1 Corinthians 16:10-14*	96
Day 39:	How to Wait Upon the Lord *1 Corinthians 16:15-24*	98

Epilogue: Moving from Glory to Glory   100

An Epiphany Journey: From Glory to Glory

O God, by the leading of a star you manifested your only Son to the peoples of the earth: Lead us, who know you now by faith, to your presence, where we may see your glory face to face; through Jesus Christ our Lord, who lives and reigns with you and the Holy Spirit, one God, now and for ever. Amen.

—*Book of Common Prayer, Collect for Epiphany*

The season of Epiphany celebrates the manifestation of Jesus Christ to the world. It reminds us of the wise men who followed the star to encounter the glory of God in the infant Jesus. Their journey was one of faith, obedience, and discovery. They left behind familiar surroundings, ventured into the unknown, and found the Savior of the world.

As we embark on this devotional journey through 1 Corinthians 12-16, we, too, are invited to a spiritual journey of transformation. We follow a greater light than the star—the Holy Spirit—who leads us from faith to greater faith, from glory to greater glory. Like the wise men, our goal is to behold the glory of Christ, not just from a distance, but face to face.

Paul's teachings in 1 Corinthians remind us that the path to this glory is rooted in love, unity, and the exercise of spiritual gifts. Each of us has been uniquely gifted to contribute to the body of Christ, to glorify God, and to build up his church. But these gifts, Paul reminds us, are meaningless without love. Love is the essence of God's glory revealed in Christ, and it is the power that transforms us into his likeness.

This devotional journey calls us to reflect on how we use our gifts and live in community as part of the body of Christ. It challenges us to embrace humility, unity, and sacrificial love, knowing that we are being prepared for the ultimate glory—to see Christ face to face.

■ Reflection:

As the wise men followed the star, how are you following the leading of God's Spirit in your life? How do your spiritual gifts reflect God's glory and prepare you for the day when you will see him face to face? Take time to pray for his guidance and transformation.

Introduction:
The Spiritual Body

What does it mean to belong to the body of Christ? How does God equip and empower His people to live as a unified, loving, and hope-filled community? In 1 Corinthians 12–16, the apostle Paul addresses these questions, offering profound insights into what it means to live as the church. This devotional series, *The Spiritual Body: Living in Unity, Love, and Resurrection Hope*, invites you to explore these themes over six weeks.

The church in Corinth was diverse, vibrant, and gifted, but it was also divided and struggling. Paul's words to them are both challenging and encouraging, reminding us that God has designed the church to be a unified body with each member playing a vital role. Whether through spiritual gifts, acts of love, or the shared hope of resurrection, God is working in and through His people for His glory.

Let's begin this series with a reminder from chapter 11: *"For those who eat and drink without discerning the body of Christ eat and drink judgment on themselves"* (1 Corinthians 11:29). This verse challenges us to recognize the body of Christ not only in the bread and wine of the Eucharist but also in the gathered community of believers. As Paul moves into chapter 12, he deepens this teaching, describing the church as a body made up of many parts. Each believer is uniquely gifted by the Holy Spirit, and every gift is essential to the health of the whole.

Chapter 13 shifts the focus to love, the foundation of all spiritual gifts. Without love, even the most extraordinary gifts are meaningless. Paul's poetic description of love challenges us to examine our hearts and seek the kind of love that reflects Christ's selflessness and grace.

In chapters 14 and 15, Paul explores the purpose of spiritual gifts in worship and proclaims the transformative power of resurrection. The gifts God gives are not for personal gain but for building up the church and pointing to the hope we have in Christ. The resurrection assures us that death is not the end, inspiring us to live boldly for the Lord. Chapter 16 provides practical examples of the Spiritual Body manifest in the personal relationships of the early church.

As you journey through these chapters, you'll discover how God calls us to live as His spiritual body. This series is an opportunity to reflect on your own gifts, relationships, and hope in Christ. Together, let us recognize the body, embrace our unity in diversity, live out love in action, and proclaim the victory of resurrection to a watching world.

Welcome to *The Spiritual Body*. May God speak to your heart and inspire you to live more fully as part of His church.

Week 1:

The Spiritual Gifts in the Body of Christ

Day 1: A Spiritual Reorientation & Test

Scripture:

"Now concerning spiritual gifts, brothers, I do not want you to be uninformed. You know that when you were pagans you were led astray to mute idols, however you were led. Therefore I want you to understand that no one speaking in the Spirit of God ever says 'Jesus is accursed!' and no one can say 'Jesus is Lord' except in the Holy Spirit." (1 Corinthians 12:1–3)

The Apostle Paul writes to the Corinthian church, addressing a community of converted pagans navigating their new faith. Before knowing Christ, they worshiped "mute idols," gods who could neither speak nor act. These idols represented a spiritual emptiness that left them blind to the truth of the one true God. Now, as Christians, their spiritual lives required reorientation, with a focus on discerning the work of the Holy Spirit and exalting Jesus Christ.

Paul saw a hunger for spiritual gifts among the Corinthians, but he also recognized a danger: their zeal for the miraculous could lead them astray if not grounded in the truth. For these new believers, spiritual experiences were not inherently signs of God's presence. Paul reminded them that not all spirits are from God. Even in their former pagan worship, they had encountered spiritual forces that were not aligned with the truth of Christ. Therefore, Paul presented a clear test for any spiritual practice or gift: Does it exalt Jesus Christ as Lord?

The phrase "Jesus is Lord" is more than a simple declaration. In Paul's time, to call Jesus "Lord" was a profound act of faith and allegiance. It acknowledged Jesus' authority as the Son of God and His supremacy over all powers and rulers, including the idols they once served. This confession could only come through the work of the Holy Spirit. Conversely, anything that dishonored Christ or diminished His lordship was not from the Spirit of God.

This teaching is as relevant today as it was for the Corinthians. In a world filled with spiritual practices, teachings, and influences, we are often bombarded by voices claiming to offer truth. Paul's guidance invites us to reorient our spiritual focus: to submit ourselves to the Holy Spirit and measure every word and action by whether it exalts Jesus.

True spiritual gifts are not about personal glory or power but about pointing others to Christ. The Holy Spirit works in and through us to magnify Jesus and build up His body, the church. When we align ourselves with the Spirit, our lives become a testimony to His lordship.

■ Reflection:

In today's world, many spiritual forces are at work. How can you use Paul's test to discern whether a spiritual influence or practice is from God? Take time to reflect on your words and actions—do they consistently exalt Jesus as Lord?

■ Prayer:

Holy Spirit, reorient my heart and mind to exalt Jesus Christ in all I say and do. Teach me to discern what is from You and to walk in submission to Your truth. May my life reflect that Jesus is Lord. Amen.

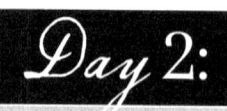 Day 2: God Desires to Empower You for the Common Good

Scripture:

"Now there are varieties of gifts, but the same Spirit; and there are varieties of service, but the same Lord; and there are varieties of activities, but it is the same God who empowers them all in everyone. To each is given the manifestation of the Spirit for the common good." (1 Corinthians 12:4–7)

Take a moment to let this truth sink in: if you are in Christ, the Holy Spirit lives in you. You are the dwelling place of God. This divine reality is both a miracle and a calling. God doesn't just dwell in you for your benefit—He has empowered you to serve, bless, and build His kingdom here on earth.

Paul's words remind us that every believer has a role in God's mission. There is no hierarchy of importance when it comes to spiritual gifts. While the gifts, services, and activities are diverse, they all come from the same God, and they all serve the same purpose: the common good of God's people. Whether your gift is teaching, serving, giving, encouraging, or something else, it comes from the Spirit and is designed to bless the church and glorify God.

The Corinthians needed this reminder because they were tempted to use their gifts for personal status or recognition. Paul refocused their attention on the giver of the gifts—God Himself. The gifts are not about personal glory but about building up the body of Christ.

This remains true for us today. Whatever God has gifted you to do, it's not for your own acclaim but for His purposes.

Consider the immense privilege of being part of God's mission. Your calling is no less important than anyone else's, no matter how public or private your role may seem. God has uniquely equipped you for the work He's prepared for you. The same Spirit that empowered the apostles, prophets, and evangelists is at work in you.

This truth calls us to two responses: gratitude and action. Gratitude for the Spirit's presence and empowerment, and action to use our gifts for the good of others. When we recognize that our spiritual gifts are meant to bless the church, share the Gospel, and expand God's kingdom, we stop striving for personal success and instead focus on serving others with love and humility.

■ Reflection:

Have you considered the divine reality that you have been given spiritual gifts by the Lord? If not, spend time in prayer today, asking God to reveal those gifts to you. How might you use them to build the body of Christ, share the Gospel, and see God's kingdom expand in this world?

■ Prayer:

Lord, thank You for the gift of Your Spirit and for empowering me to serve You. Reveal the gifts You have given me, and teach me to use them faithfully for the good of others and the glory of Your name. Amen.

Day 3: God's Prerogative in the Giving of Gifts

Scripture:

"For to one is given through the Spirit the utterance of wisdom, and to another the utterance of knowledge according to the same Spirit, to another faith by the same Spirit, to another gifts of healing by the one Spirit, to another the working of miracles, to another prophecy, to another the ability to distinguish between spirits, to another various kinds of tongues, to another the interpretation of tongues. All these are empowered by one and the same Spirit, who apportions to each one individually as he wills."
(1 Corinthians 12:8–11)

Fairness is one of the earliest and most enduring concepts we wrestle with in life. How often do we, like children, cry out, "That's not fair!"—whether in response to a situation we don't understand or something we feel we've missed out on. But what if God's plan for our lives is not about fairness, but about goodness?

Paul's teaching on spiritual gifts reminds us of a profound truth: God distributes gifts as *He wills*. The gifts of the Spirit are not handed out equally, nor are they the same for everyone. Instead, the Spirit gives to each person individually according to His divine wisdom and purpose. Some are gifted with the ability to teach, others with discernment, still others with healing, prophecy, or tongues. The list is long and varied, and the distribution is intentional.

Why is this important? Because the diversity of gifts reflects the beauty of God's design for His church. If we all had the same gifts, the body of Christ would lack the balance and richness necessary for its mission. Each gift contributes something unique to the work of the Spirit, and every role is essential for the flourishing of the whole.

Yet, it can be easy to compare our gifts to others and feel inadequate or even envious. Why does she get the gift of teaching while I'm left with something less visible? Why does he have the faith to move mountains when I struggle to believe? Paul's reminder to the Corinthians—and to us—is that all gifts come from the same Spirit and are empowered by the same God. The value of a gift is not in how it compares to others, but in the fact that it comes from God and serves His purpose.

Today, embrace the gifts God has given you. Trust in His perfect wisdom and plan. Delight in the variety of gifts He has given to His people and resist the temptation to compare or covet. Instead, use your gifts to bless others and glorify God. In doing so, you reflect the unity and diversity of the body of Christ, working together under the guidance of one Spirit.

■ Reflection:

Have you considered the variety of gifts God gives His people? Reflect on the gift(s) God has given you. Are you using them joyfully, or are you longing for something different? Ask God to help you delight in His gifts and to use them faithfully for His kingdom.

■ Prayer:

Lord, thank You for the gifts You have given me and to others in Your church. Teach me to trust Your wisdom and to use my gifts for Your glory. Help me to celebrate the gifts of others and work in harmony with them to build Your kingdom. Amen.

Day 4: Unity and Equality in the Body of Christ

Scripture:

"For just as the body is one and has many members, and all the members of the body, though many, are one body, so it is with Christ. For in one Spirit we were all baptized into one body—Jews or Greeks, slaves or free—and all were made to drink of one Spirit." (1 Corinthians 12:12–13)

Unity is at the heart of God's design for His church. In just two sentences, Paul repeats the word "one" five times, emphasizing the foundational truth that in Christ, we are one body, united by one Spirit. Before Christ, the world was divided by barriers like ethnicity, status, and religion. But through His redemptive work, Jesus broke down those walls. Now, regardless of background, we are united as children of God, one in the body of Christ.

To help the Corinthians grasp this truth, Paul uses the human body as a metaphor. Just as a body has many parts, each with a unique function, so does the church. Each member of the body of Christ plays a vital role, contributing to the health and mission of the whole. This unity is not something we create; it is a gift from God, given through baptism and the Holy Spirit.

In baptism, we renounce our old ways and embrace a new life in Christ. The waters of baptism wash away our sin and mark us as members of one family. This act of grace is universal—every believer, regardless of their past, is equally in need of God's mercy. Through baptism, we are reconciled to God and to one another.

Our shared dependence on Christ's grace humbles us and binds us together as one people.

But unity does not erase diversity. In the body of Christ, we bring our unique gifts, backgrounds, and perspectives, not to compete but to complement one another. The Spirit empowers us to see one another not as rivals but as brothers and sisters in Christ. Together, we form a body that reflects God's glory—one that values every member equally and works together for His purposes.

In a human body, no part can function alone. Walking requires feet, legs, arms for balance, and even eyes for direction. Similarly, the church thrives when its members work in harmony. Some cast vision, others organize plans, some preach, some pray, and others serve. Every role is crucial, and every person is valued.

Today, reflect on the unity and equality that come through Christ. Where do you see disunity or inequality in the church? How might God be calling you to bridge those gaps? Through the Spirit, we are empowered to embrace our differences and celebrate our shared identity in Christ. Let us work together as one body to glorify Him.

■ Reflection:

Where do you see disunity or inequality in your church today? How might God be calling you to use your gifts to bridge those gaps or encourage His people?

■ Prayer:

Lord, thank You for uniting us as one body through Your Spirit. Teach me to value every member of Your church and to use my gifts to build unity. May we reflect Your love and grace in all we do. Amen.

Day 5: Breaking the Bondage of Pride and Insecurity

Scripture:

"For the body does not consist of one member but of many. If the foot should say, 'Because I am not a hand, I do not belong to the body,' that would not make it any less a part of the body. And if the ear should say, 'Because I am not an eye, I do not belong to the body,' that would not make it any less a part of the body. If the whole body were an eye, where would be the sense of hearing? If the whole body were an ear, where would be the sense of smell? But as it is, God arranged the members in the body, each one of them, as he chose." 1 Corinthians 12:14-18

If comparison wasn't an issue before social media, it certainly is now. Platforms like Facebook and Instagram encourage us to compare everything from vacations to children—even our dogs! But let's be clear: that was never God's intent. God isn't against social media itself, but He does call us to live in unity and harmony. Comparison, however, breeds unhealthy judgment, envy, and division.

Psalm 139 reveals the intimate care God took in creating you: *"You knit me together in my mother's womb"* (v. 13). Unlike us, God has no bad days. When He was designing you, He wasn't distracted or tired. You are His masterpiece, created intentionally and with great care. Ephesians 2:10 reminds us that you are His workmanship, created for good works that God prepared in advance for you to do. Everything about you has been designed to work in sync with His Spirit.

In God's eyes, no one is greater or lesser. We are all indispensable parts of His body. Those you envy? You need them. Those you look down upon? You need them too. Pride and insecurity have no place in the body of Christ because, as Paul writes, *"God arranged the members in the body, each one of them, as He chose"* (v. 18).

God's design for His church is one of mutual interdependence. Problems arise when we resist this truth—when we compare, resent, or separate ourselves from others. Unity and harmony in the body of Christ begin with the recognition that each member is equally valuable, uniquely gifted, and purposefully placed.

■ *Reflection:*

Take time today to repent of comparing yourself to others—whether in pride or insecurity. Ask the Lord to show you how He wants you to give to and receive from His body. Remember: you belong in the body of Christ. You are wanted, needed, and deeply loved.

■ *Prayer:*

Heavenly Father, thank You for creating me with purpose and intention. Forgive me for the times I have compared myself to others, whether in pride or insecurity. Help me to see myself and others as You see us—uniquely made, deeply loved, and essential to Your body. Teach me how to walk in unity and harmony with my brothers and sisters in Christ. Show me how to use the gifts You have given me for Your glory and to build up Your church. May I celebrate the gifts of others and embrace the beautiful plan You have for us to work together. In Jesus' name, I pray. Amen.

Day 6: One Body of Christ

Scripture:

"If all were a single member, where would the body be? As it is, there are many parts, yet one body. The eye cannot say to the hand, 'I have no need of you,' nor again the head to the feet, 'I have no need of you.' On the contrary, the parts of the body that seem to be weaker are indispensable... If one member suffers, all suffer together; if one member is honored, all rejoice together." (1 Corinthians 12:19–26)

When my husband and I first started ministry, we met José, a janitor at our large Episcopal church. José worked quietly and faithfully, often whistling hymns or humming softly as he went about his duties. He had a warm and gentle demeanor, the kind of presence that made people feel at peace. We saw him as the perfect janitor—hardworking, kind, and dependable. What we didn't realize was that José's influence extended far beyond the church building.

One day, José shared with us his true passion: planting churches. After finishing his work at the church, José would go out into the community, especially to places where brokenness and need were most apparent. He explained his simple method: he looked for people who were hurting, shared the Gospel with them, and invited them to gather with others to learn about Jesus.

This wasn't a one-time occurrence. Over time, José would watch as a handful of people became a growing community of believers. Once the group was well-established—sometimes numbering 50, 100, or more—José would identify a new leader to shepherd the church and move on to plant another. He repeated this process again and again.

When my husband asked him how many churches he had planted, José paused and began counting. He quietly listed them off, one by one, until he finally said, "At least five." Five churches! Without formal theological training, a seminary degree, or a public platform, José had faithfully built the kingdom of God in ways that many could only dream of.

What stood out most about José was his humility. He didn't boast about his work. He didn't seek recognition or accolades. He simply followed God's call with quiet faith and determination, trusting that his obedience would bear fruit. While many saw him only as a janitor, God saw him as a faithful servant, honoring him for his dedication to the Gospel and his love for others.

José's story beautifully illustrates Paul's message in 1 Corinthians 12. In the body of Christ, there are no insignificant roles. The parts of the body that seem weaker or less honorable are often the ones God uses most powerfully. José's janitorial work was as much a ministry as his church planting, and his life reminds us that every act of faithfulness—whether visible or hidden—matters deeply to God.

■ Reflection:

How are you inspired by José's story of faithfulness and humility? Are there people in your church whose work you've overlooked or undervalued? How can you honor their contributions and encourage them today?

■ Prayer:

Lord, thank You for servants like José who faithfully live out Your calling, no matter the role or recognition. Teach me to value every member of the body of Christ and to serve You with humility and joy. May my life bring You glory in all I do. Amen.

Day 7: Do You Desire the Higher Gifts?

Scripture:

"Now you are the body of Christ and individually members of it. And God has appointed in the church first apostles, second prophets, third teachers, then miracles, then gifts of healing, helping, administrating, and various kinds of tongues. Are all apostles? Are all prophets? Are all teachers? Do all work miracles? Do all possess gifts of healing? Do all speak with tongues? Do all interpret? But earnestly desire the higher gifts. And I will show you a still more excellent way." (1 Corinthians 12:27–31)

Do you desire the higher gifts? What do you believe makes a gift "higher"? For the Corinthians, the higher gifts were those that brought attention, applause, and recognition—the "showy" gifts. They admired apostles, prophets, and miracle workers because their work was visible and dramatic. But as Paul reminds them, spiritual gifts are not about self-glorification or personal recognition; they are about glorifying Christ and building up His church.

Paul acknowledges the roles of apostles, prophets, teachers, and others, but he never separates them in value or significance. All spiritual gifts come from the same Spirit and serve the same purpose: to exalt Jesus and edify the body of Christ. The Corinthians had missed this point, becoming focused on status rather than service.

Paul's rhetorical questions make it clear that no one has every gift, and no gift is sufficient on its own. The church functions as one body, with each part fulfilling a unique and indispensable role.

Apostles proclaim the Gospel and establish churches, prophets speak God's truth, teachers build understanding, and those with gifts of healing and miracles display God's power. Helping and administrating may seem less "glamorous," but they mobilize the church to act with compassion and order. Even speaking in tongues, a gift the Corinthians highly valued, serves its purpose only when it builds others up through interpretation.

The higher gifts Paul mentions are not about status but about purpose. A higher gift is one that most effectively builds up the body of Christ and glorifies God in a particular moment. The true measure of any spiritual gift is not its visibility but its motivation. Is it exercised out of love for God and others? Does it glorify Jesus and edify His church?

In the final verse, Paul introduces a "still more excellent way." This sets the stage for chapter 13, where he reveals that love is the foundation of all spiritual gifts. Without love, even the most dramatic and impressive gifts are meaningless.

■ Reflection:

Do you consider certain spiritual gifts to be higher or more important than others? If so, why? Do you eagerly desire those gifts for God's glory or for personal recognition? How can you continue to use Paul's spiritual gift test: does it glorify God and edify the body of Christ?

■ Prayer:

Lord, thank You for the gifts You have given to Your church. Teach me to value all gifts and to use mine in a way that glorifies You and builds up Your people. Help me to seek the more excellent way of love, so that everything I do reflects Your grace and truth. Amen.

Week 2:

Love, the More Excellent Way

Day 8: Spiritual Gifts Require Spiritual Maturity

Scripture:

"If I speak in the tongues of men and of angels, but have not love, I am a noisy gong or a clanging cymbal. And if I have prophetic powers, and understand all mysteries and all knowledge, and if I have all faith, so as to remove mountains, but have not love, I am nothing. If I give away all I have, and if I deliver up my body to be burned, but have not love, I gain nothing." (1 Corinthians 13:1–3)

The Corinthians loved spiritual gifts. They admired the miraculous, the impressive, and the showy demonstrations of power that made them feel important. But as Paul transitions into one of the most profound chapters in Scripture, he challenges their—and our—entire approach to spirituality. His point is simple and piercing: spiritual gifts, no matter how extraordinary, are worthless without love.

This chapter forces us to consider the deeper question: *Are we spiritually mature?* Maturity in Christ is not measured by the gifts we possess or the actions we perform but by the love that motivates us. Gifts like speaking in tongues, prophesying, and faith to move mountains can inspire awe, but without love, they amount to nothing more than noise and emptiness. Even extreme acts of self-sacrifice, such as giving away everything or facing martyrdom, are meaningless if they are not rooted in love.

Paul's teaching echoes the words of Jesus: *"Not everyone who says to me, 'Lord, Lord,' will enter the kingdom of heaven... On that day many will say to me, 'Lord, Lord, did we not prophesy in your name, and cast out demons in your name, and do many mighty works in your name?"* (Matthew 7:21–22). Both Jesus and Paul remind us that what truly matters is not the works themselves but the heart behind them. Love is the ultimate measure of spiritual maturity.

This passage challenges us to examine our own motivations. Why do we serve? Why do we use our gifts? Is it to receive recognition, to feel important, or to impress others? Or is it out of genuine love for God and His people? Love must be the driving force behind everything we do in the body of Christ.

Paul's words are not just convicting; they are also deeply hopeful. They remind us that love is both a gift and a calling. God's love for us is the foundation of everything. As we grow in awareness of His love, it transforms us, enabling us to love others in return. True spiritual maturity flows from this love—love that glorifies God and edifies His people.

■ *Reflection:*

How are you doing with love? Do you live as one deeply loved by God, allowing that love to overflow into love for others? Spend time with the Lord today, asking Him to fill you with His love so that everything you do is rooted in Him.

■ *Prayer:*

Lord, thank You for loving me unconditionally. Help me to grow in spiritual maturity by abiding in Your love. Teach me to love You with all my heart and to reflect Your love to others in all I do. May my gifts and actions always glorify You and build up Your church. Amen.

Day 9: The Full Expression of Love

Scripture:

"Love is patient and kind; love does not envy or boast; it is not arrogant or rude. It does not insist on its own way; it is not irritable or resentful; it does not rejoice at wrongdoing, but rejoices with the truth. Love bears all things, believes all things, hopes all things, endures all things." (1 Corinthians 13:4–7)

Paul's description of love is one of the most well-known passages in the Bible, but it's far more than a poetic ideal. It is a call to live out the kind of love that God demonstrates toward us. As Paul teaches the Corinthians about spiritual gifts, he reveals the purpose behind those gifts: they are given in love and are to be used for love. And the ultimate example of love is Jesus Himself.

When we examine the life of Jesus, we see the full expression of the love Paul describes. Jesus was patient and kind with His disciples, even when they misunderstood Him, doubted Him, or betrayed Him. He never envied others or boasted in His power, even though He had every reason to do so. He was humble, never rude, and He didn't insist on His own way—even as He prayed in Gethsemane, "Not my will, but yours be done."

Jesus wasn't irritable or resentful, even when His plans were interrupted or when He faced hostility from those who should have welcomed Him. He always rejoiced in the truth, glorifying His Father in everything He did. And above all, Jesus bore the ultimate burden on the cross, enduring suffering and shame for the sake of love.

Jesus is the perfect example of this divine love, and His love makes it possible for us to love others. Paul's desire for the Corinthians—and for us—is that we would be transformed by God's love so that we can reflect that love in our relationships. But this transformation doesn't come from striving or self-effort; it comes from receiving God's love through Jesus Christ.

When we soak in the truth of God's love for us, it changes everything. It gives us the patience to bear with others, the kindness to serve them, and the humility to put their needs ahead of our own. God's love equips us to rejoice in the truth, to forgive, and to endure difficult relationships or situations.

Today, let yourself rest in the knowledge that you are deeply loved by God. Let His love shape your heart, soften your edges, and prepare you to be a conduit of His love to the world around you.

■ Reflection:

Spend time today reflecting on the love of the Lord for you. How has His love transformed you? How does He want to continue shaping you and loving others through you?

■ Prayer:

Jesus, thank You for being the perfect expression of love. Help me to receive Your love fully and allow it to transform me. Teach me to love as You love, so that I may glorify You and build up others in all I do. Amen.

Day 10: An Eternal Focus

Scripture:

"Love never ends. As for prophecies, they will pass away; as for tongues, they will cease; as for knowledge, it will pass away. For we know in part and we prophesy in part, but when the perfect comes, the partial will pass away." (1 Corinthians 13:8–10)

The Apostle Paul calls the Corinthians—and us—to lift our eyes beyond the temporary and focus on what is eternal. While the Corinthians were captivated by spiritual gifts like prophecy, tongues, and knowledge, Paul reminds them that these gifts are for the here and now, not forever. Spiritual gifts are tools for building the church in this imperfect world. But one day, when Christ returns and we see Him face to face, those tools will no longer be needed.

Paul explains that spiritual gifts are partial and temporary. They serve a vital purpose in this "now but not yet" phase of God's kingdom. Now, we live in a world where faith must be built, the Gospel must be shared, and the church must be strengthened. But when the perfect comes—when God's kingdom is fully realized— our understanding will no longer be partial. We will know fully and love perfectly, just as we are fully known and perfectly loved by God.

What remains forever is love. "Love never ends" because God, the source of all true love, is eternal. While spiritual gifts have an expiration date, love does not. Love is the essence of God's character and will be the defining reality of His kingdom for eternity. In that glorious future, we won't need prophecies, tongues, or special knowledge because we will experience the fullness of God's love directly.

For now, Paul encourages us to use the gifts God has given us with an eternal focus. These gifts are important, but they are not the goal. They are a foretaste of what is to come. They remind us that this life is a preparation for something far greater. As C.S. Lewis beautifully wrote in *Mere Christianity*, *"If I find in myself desires which nothing in this world can satisfy, the only logical explanation is that I was made for another world."* You were made for another world—a world where love reigns supreme and all things are made new.

Paul challenges us to live with eternity in mind, practicing love as the foundation for all we do. Spiritual gifts are tools, but love is the purpose. As we exercise our gifts, let us remember that they are temporary expressions of God's eternal love, pointing us and others toward His kingdom.

■ *Reflection:*

How do you keep perspective on what is temporary and eternal? Take time today to reflect on Lewis's words: "You were made for another world." How do your deepest desires reveal that the perfect has not yet come?

■ *Prayer:*

Lord, thank You for the gifts You've given to build Your church and display Your glory. Help me to focus on what is eternal, to live and serve with love, and to look forward with hope to the day when I will know and experience Your perfect love fully. Amen.

Day 11: The Most Excellent Way

Scripture:

"When I was a child, I spoke like a child, I thought like a child, I reasoned like a child. When I became a man, I gave up childish ways. For now we see in a mirror dimly, but then face to face. Now I know in part; then I shall know fully, even as I have been fully known. So now faith, hope, and love abide, these three; but the greatest of these is love." (1 Corinthians 13:11–13)

If the pandemic has taught us anything, it's the value of presence. Video calls and online gatherings have been blessings in times of separation, but they cannot replace the joy of being physically present with loved ones. Deep within, we know that seeing someone through a screen is not the same as being with them face to face.

Paul draws on this innate human longing to stir up a similar yearning in the Corinthian believers—not to see people, but to see the Lord face to face. He likens our current understanding of God to looking into a dim mirror, where the reflection is helpful but incomplete. Just as a mirror can only reveal part of who we are, our current knowledge of God is partial.

Through Jesus, the Holy Spirit, and Scripture, we catch glimpses of God's character, love, and glory. Yet these glimpses are but shadows of the fullness that awaits us. The Christian hope is that one day, we will see God in His glory, fully and completely. On that day, the dim mirror will be replaced by a direct, face-to-face encounter with the One who created us, redeemed us, and loves us more than we can comprehend.

As we wait for that day, Paul reminds us that we are in a process of spiritual growth. Like children maturing into adults, we are growing in our understanding of God and His ways. Through prayer, Scripture, worship, and fellowship, we come to know Him more deeply and reflect His image more fully (2 Corinthians 3:17–18). But even in our greatest moments of clarity, there is still more to God than we can currently grasp.

This anticipation of seeing God face to face should inspire us to live in faith, hope, and love. Faith sustains us as we trust in what we cannot yet fully see. Hope anchors us as we wait for the day when all will be revealed. But love—the greatest of these—is what ties it all together. Love is eternal because it reflects God's very nature. Love will remain even when faith and hope are no longer needed, for in His presence, all will be fulfilled.

■ *Reflection:*

What do you feel when you think about seeing the Lord face to face and knowing Him fully, just as He knows you? Let that longing stir your heart today. It is the Spirit within you, pointing toward the culmination of His kingdom.

■ *Prayer:*

Lord, thank You for the hope of seeing You face to face. Grow my faith and hope as I wait for that day, and deepen my love for You and for others. Teach me to live with eternity in my heart, reflecting Your love in all I do. Come, Lord Jesus, come! Amen.

Day 12: Do You Need Some Spiritual Redirection?

Scripture:

"Pursue love, and earnestly desire the spiritual gifts, especially that you may prophesy. For one who speaks in a tongue speaks not to men but to God; for no one understands him, but he utters mysteries in the Spirit. On the other hand, the one who prophesies speaks to people for their upbuilding and encouragement and consolation. The one who speaks in a tongue builds up himself, but the one who prophesies builds up the church. Now I want you all to speak in tongues, but even more to prophesy. The one who prophesies is greater than the one who speaks in tongues, unless someone interprets, so that the church may be built up."
(1 Corinthians 14:1–5)

Paul's words to the Corinthians provide a much-needed redirection. Their excitement over spiritual gifts, especially speaking in tongues, had shifted their focus away from God and others and onto themselves. Like kindergarteners buzzing with excitement before a field trip to the zoo, their energy was consuming but misdirected. The result was a church captivated by self-promotion rather than service.

Paul challenges their priorities, calling them to grow beyond their childish ways. He reminds them of the true purpose of spiritual gifts: to exalt Jesus Christ and build up the body of Christ. Speaking in tongues, while a legitimate gift, primarily edifies the individual. Paul doesn't discourage its practice but urges the Corinthians to desire gifts that build others up—especially prophecy.

Prophecy, in this context, involves speaking God's truth to the church in a way that encourages, comforts, and strengthens. Unlike tongues, which require interpretation, prophecy communicates directly and clearly for the benefit of all. Paul's desire is clear: spiritual gifts should foster unity and growth in the church, not elevate individuals or create division.

This teaching is just as relevant today. How often do we approach worship or church participation with a consumer mindset, asking, "What will I get out of this?" rather than, "How can I contribute to this?" Corporate worship is not about personal gain but about glorifying God and building up His people. When we focus solely on ourselves, we miss the opportunity to experience the beauty of interdependence—the flourishing that comes when each member brings their unique gifts to serve the whole.

Paul's redirection reminds us to evaluate our hearts and priorities. Are we seeking gifts or roles in the church for recognition, or are we using what God has given us to bless others? True spiritual maturity is marked by love—a love that puts others first and seeks the good of the entire body.

■ *Reflection:*

How do you view corporate worship? Do you come with the purpose of exalting Jesus Christ and building up His people, or are you focused on what you will receive? Ask God to redirect your heart and show you how to bring your gifts to serve His body.

■ *Prayer:*

Lord, thank You for the gifts You have given to build up Your church. Teach me to use them with love, focusing on exalting You and serving others. Redirect my heart when it strays toward self-centeredness, and help me to be a faithful and humble part of Your body. Amen.

Day 13: The Body of Christ Is Meant to Live in Harmony

Scripture:

"Now, brothers, if I come to you speaking in tongues, how will I benefit you unless I bring you some revelation or knowledge or prophecy or teaching? If even lifeless instruments, such as the flute or the harp, do not give distinct notes, how will anyone know what is played? And if the bugle gives an indistinct sound, who will get ready for battle?" (1 Corinthians 14:6–8)

Have you ever been to a concert where the music seemed to lift your soul to heavenly places? Contrast that with a children's recital where the notes are off, the rhythm is shaky, and the harmony is nonexistent. While there's charm in the learning process, disharmony can be grating.

Paul addresses a similar issue of disharmony within the Corinthian church. Their worship gatherings had become chaotic, dominated by speaking in tongues that few, if any, could understand. Instead of edifying the body of Christ, these displays created confusion. Worship, meant to unify and glorify God, was disrupted by what Paul describes as indistinct sounds—like musical instruments played without purpose or coordination.

Paul uses a bugle as an example. In battle, a bugle's distinct notes were used to signal commands. If the sound was unclear, soldiers wouldn't know whether to advance or retreat. Similarly, in worship, the words and actions of the congregation must be intelligible and purposeful so that all are strengthened in faith and encouraged in their walk with Christ.

Speaking in tongues is a gift from God, intended for personal prayer and connection with Him. However, Paul emphasizes that corporate worship is a time for building up the entire body. Without interpretation, tongues bring no benefit to the gathered church. Instead, Paul urges believers to focus on gifts like prophecy, teaching, and knowledge—gifts that communicate God's truth clearly and directly for the edification of all.

The heart of Paul's message is this: worship is not about individual expression but about the collective harmony of God's people. Just as an orchestra works together to create beautiful music, the body of Christ must work together in worship to glorify God and strengthen one another.

For worship to be harmonious, every member has a role to play. We lift our voices in song, we listen attentively to God's Word, and we pray for and with one another. Each of these actions brings unity and builds the church.

■ *Reflection:*

How is your time in corporate worship strengthening your faith? Likewise, how is your participation in worship edifying the larger body of Christ? Consider how you can contribute to the harmony and purpose of worship in your church.

■ *Prayer:*

Lord, thank You for the gift of corporate worship. Help me to approach worship with a heart that seeks to glorify You and edify others. Teach me to use my gifts in harmony with Your people, so that together we may create a beautiful offering of praise to You. Amen.

Day 14: Are You Speaking in a Foreign Language?

Scripture:

"So with yourselves, if with your tongue you utter speech that is not intelligible, how will anyone know what is said? For you will be speaking into the air. There are doubtless many different languages in the world, and none is without meaning, but if I do not know the meaning of the language, I will be a foreigner to the speaker and the speaker a foreigner to me. So with yourselves, since you are eager for manifestations of the Spirit, strive to excel in building up the church." (1 Corinthians 14:9–12)

Imagine being in a room where everyone is speaking a language you don't understand. While the sounds might be interesting, the conversation is meaningless to you. This is the analogy Paul uses to explain the inappropriate use of tongues in the Corinthian church. When spiritual gifts are exercised without consideration for others, they become empty noise, offering no benefit to the listener or the community.

Paul's concern wasn't about whether speaking in tongues was legitimate—it is a gift of the Spirit—but about how and when it was used. The Corinthians were eager for manifestations of the Spirit, but their enthusiasm had led to chaos and confusion in worship. People were speaking in tongues with no interpretation, creating an atmosphere where the congregation could neither understand nor be edified.

Paul reminds the Corinthians—and us—that the purpose of spiritual gifts is to build up the church, not to showcase individual spirituality. Intelligibility matters because worship is about more than personal expression; it's about mutual edification. This is why Paul prioritizes prophecy, a gift that communicates God's truth clearly and directly for the encouragement, strengthening, and consolation of the whole body.

Paul's example also challenges us to consider how we communicate within the church and with those outside it. Are we speaking in ways that are clear and understandable, or do we unintentionally create barriers? This isn't just about languages; it's about making the Gospel accessible. Sometimes, even within the church, we use "insider" language or theological terms that can confuse or alienate others. Our goal should always be to communicate God's truth in a way that everyone can understand and respond to.

Paul's reminder is as relevant today as it was in Corinth. Spiritual gifts are not for personal glory but for the good of the body. When exercised in love and with clarity, they reflect God's presence and purpose, strengthening the church and drawing others to Him.

■ *Reflection:*

How do you feel when you hear someone speaking in a language you don't understand? How does that experience help you appreciate the importance of intelligibility in worship? Consider whether you are communicating God's Word in ways that are clear and accessible to others, both inside and outside the church.

■ *Prayer:*

Lord, thank You for the gifts You've given to Your church. Help me to use them in ways that build up Your people and make Your truth clear to all. Teach me to speak with love, wisdom, and understanding, so that I may reflect Your heart and glorify Your name. Amen.

# Week 3:

Building Up the Body in Love

Day 15: Private Versus Corporate Expressions of Prayer and Praise

Scripture:

"Therefore, one who speaks in a tongue should pray that he may interpret. For if I pray in a tongue, my spirit prays but my mind is unfruitful. What am I to do? I will pray with my spirit, but I will pray with my mind also; I will sing praise with my spirit, but I will sing with my mind also." (1 Corinthians 14:13–15)

Paul's "therefore" in this passage signals an important connection between his previous teaching and his practical application. He has just reminded the Corinthians to *"strive to excel in building up the church"* (v. 12). Now, he explains how to live out that principle by distinguishing between private and corporate expressions of prayer and praise.

Speaking or praying in tongues is a gift that allows the spirit to connect with God on a deep, spiritual level. It can be a beautiful way to commune with the Lord, but Paul emphasizes the need for discernment in its use. In private prayer and praise, tongues can be freely expressed because it builds up the individual believer. However, in corporate worship, tongues must be accompanied by interpretation to ensure that the whole congregation is edified.

This distinction highlights a key principle: private spiritual practices are for personal edification, while corporate worship is for building up the body of Christ. Both are essential, but they serve different purposes. In private, you can pray and sing with your spirit, letting your heart overflow in worship without needing to explain or interpret. However, when gathered with others, Paul encourages praying and praising with both spirit and mind, ensuring that your worship builds up the faith of those around you.

Paul's teaching also serves as a reminder that private and corporate spiritual disciplines should complement each other. Praying in tongues or engaging in personal worship doesn't replace the need for other spiritual practices, such as studying Scripture, hearing God's Word preached, or worshiping with the body of Christ. Likewise, corporate worship should not be the only time we engage with God. Both private and public expressions are vital for a balanced and mature faith.

Since Covid, many believers have leaned heavily on private worship and prayer, often neglecting the communal aspect of faith. While private communion with the Lord is essential, it's equally important to gather with others, praying and praising in ways that edify the larger body.

■ Reflection:

How do you nurture and exercise your private communion with the Lord? What about your participation in corporate prayer and praise? Ask the Lord to reveal whether you have a proper balance between the two and how you can better contribute to building up His church.

■ Prayer:

Lord, thank You for the gift of private communion with You and the joy of corporate worship with Your people. Help me to discern when to pray and praise in private and when to focus on edifying the church. Teach me to honor You in both settings, building my faith and strengthening the body of Christ. Amen.

Day 16: It Is Not About You!

Scripture:

"Otherwise, if you give thanks with your spirit, how can anyone in the position of an outsider say 'Amen' to your thanksgiving when he does not know what you are saying? For you may be giving thanks well enough, but the other person is not being built up." (1 Corinthians 14:16–17)

Paul's words to the Corinthians cut to the heart of an issue that is all too common: the tendency to make worship about ourselves. The Corinthians were so caught up in their spiritual experiences, particularly speaking in tongues, that they had lost sight of the purpose of corporate worship: to glorify God and edify the body of Christ.

This self-centered approach to worship is not unique to the Corinthians. How often do we walk into church focused on what we will get out of it—whether it's the music, the sermon, or even the social interactions? Paul's reminder is as relevant today as it was then: worship is not about you.

Rick Warren captured this truth perfectly in the opening line of *The Purpose Driven Life:* "It is not about you." These words remind us to shift our focus outward—toward God and others. Worship is a communal experience where the body of Christ gathers to give thanks, glorify God, and build each other up. When we make it all about us, we lose the heart of what worship is meant to be.

Paul's point is practical and logical. If you are giving thanks to God in a way that others cannot understand, how can they join you in saying "Amen"? Worship is not just an individual act; it is meant to be shared. The words and actions we bring to corporate worship should be clear, intelligible, and inclusive, allowing others to participate and be encouraged.

This principle extends beyond Sunday morning services. When we carry the mindset of "It's not about you" into our daily lives, we begin to reflect Christ's love more fully. In our homes, workplaces, and communities, this shift in focus allows us to invest in others, prioritize their needs, and build relationships that glorify God.

The truth is, Christians often struggle to live this out consistently. As Paul implies, self-centeredness can hinder the kingdom of God. But when we embrace the call to focus on God and others, we become the kind of witnesses who draw people to Him.

■ Reflection:

Let those words sink in: *"It is not about you."* How can embracing this truth transform your presence in worship, at home, at work, or in your community? Reflect on ways this mindset can help you better build the kingdom of God.

■ Prayer:

Lord, thank You for the gift of worship and the body of Christ. Help me to remember that it is not about me but about glorifying You and building up others. Teach me to reflect Your love in all I do, putting others before myself and investing in Your kingdom. Amen.

Day 17: Two Extreme Views of the Spiritual Gifts

Scripture:

"I thank God that I speak in tongues more than all of you. Nevertheless, in church I would rather speak five words with my mind in order to instruct others, than ten thousand words in a tongue." (1 Corinthians 14:18–19)

Paul's words here strike a delicate balance in the conversation about spiritual gifts. He openly affirms his practice of speaking in tongues, a gift he deeply values and uses in his personal spiritual life. Yet, he also prioritizes clarity and edification in the context of corporate worship. This balance speaks to two extreme views of spiritual gifts that persist today: an overemphasis on the gifts or a complete dismissal of them.

On one hand, there are those who are overly focused on spiritual gifts, particularly speaking in tongues. For some, this gift becomes a marker of spiritual maturity or even salvation. This approach can foster division, pride, and confusion within the church—much like it did in Corinth. Paul's teaching challenges this mindset. While he valued the gift of tongues, he consistently emphasized that gifts are not for self-glorification but for building up the church.

On the other hand, there are those who believe that spiritual gifts ceased with the apostles and are no longer relevant today. This cessationist view can lead to a faith that dismisses the active work of the Holy Spirit in and through believers. Yet, Scripture consistently points to the ongoing presence and power of the Spirit in the life of the church.

Paul offers a middle ground: affirming the value of spiritual gifts while calling for discernment and maturity in their use. Speaking in tongues, for example, is a beautiful gift for personal prayer and communion with God. Paul himself practiced it regularly. But in a corporate setting, he prioritized clear, intelligible communication that would edify others. *"I would rather speak five words with my mind in order to instruct others, than ten thousand words in a tongue."*

This principle applies to all spiritual gifts. Gifts are meant to exalt Christ and strengthen His body, not to elevate the individual exercising them. Spiritual maturity means knowing when and how to use your gifts in a way that serves God's purposes and blesses His people.

For believers today, the challenge is to approach spiritual gifts with both openness and discernment. Are you overly focused on certain gifts, or are you dismissing them altogether? Paul's example invites us to seek the Spirit's work in our lives while keeping love and edification at the center.

■ *Reflection:*

Where do you fall on the spectrum of views regarding spiritual gifts? Are you open to the Holy Spirit's work in your life, or do you approach the gifts with hesitation or skepticism? Ask God to guide you in understanding and using His gifts with love and maturity.

■ *Prayer:*

Holy Spirit, thank You for Your presence and gifts in my life. Help me to approach spiritual gifts with humility, love, and discernment. Teach me to use them in ways that glorify Christ and build up His church. Open my heart to Your work and guide me in spiritual maturity. Amen.

Day 18: Grow Up in the Lord!

Scripture:

"Brothers, do not be children in your thinking. Be infants in evil, but in your thinking be mature. In the Law it is written, 'By people of strange tongues and by the lips of foreigners will I speak to this people, and even then they will not listen to me, says the Lord.' Thus tongues are a sign not for believers but for unbelievers, while prophecy is a sign not for unbelievers but for believers."
(1 Corinthians 14:20–22)

The Apostle Paul never shied away from hard truths. In his letters to the Corinthians, he repeatedly called them out for their spiritual immaturity. While they were eager to embrace spiritual gifts, especially the gift of tongues, they often used them in ways that were self-serving and disorderly. Paul's challenge was simple but profound: *Grow up in the Lord!*

Paul contrasts two ways of living: being infants in evil and being mature in thought. To be an "infant in evil" means to still be innocent and untainted by sin. This is a good and holy aspiration. However, Paul warns that their thinking about spiritual matters must grow beyond childishness. While their excitement about spiritual gifts was not inherently wrong, their behavior revealed a lack of maturity. Worship had become more about performance and competition than about glorifying God and edifying the church.

Paul references Isaiah's prophecy to drive his point home. In Isaiah 28:11-12, the prophet warns Israel that their disobedience would lead to judgment. That judgment would come in the form of foreign invaders speaking languages they could not understand. For Israel, the sound of strange tongues was a reminder of their failure to listen to God. Paul uses this to warn the Corinthians: tongues are not always a sign of God's blessing but can be a sign of His judgment.

This context should have humbled the Corinthians. Rather than celebrating their ability to speak in tongues as proof of their spiritual status, they needed to reflect on whether their use of the gift glorified God and edified others. Paul calls them to mature in their faith, to steward their gifts wisely, and to prioritize the edification of the church above all else.

This challenge applies to us as well. Spiritual maturity is not just about acquiring knowledge or practicing gifts—it's about growing in love, humility, and a Christ-centered focus. When we mature in faith, we learn to use our gifts in ways that reflect God's character and serve His people.

■ *Reflection:*

How is the Lord inviting you to grow in maturity today? Are there areas of your faith where you've remained childlike in thought or action? Reflect on how spiritual growth can help you use your gifts more faithfully for God's glory and the good of His church.

■ *Prayer:*

Lord, thank You for the gifts You've given me and for the invitation to grow in You. Help me to mature in my faith, leaving behind childish ways and embracing Your wisdom. Teach me to use my gifts with love and humility, always seeking to glorify You and edify Your people. Amen.

Day 19: The Faithful Practice of Spiritual Gifts

Scripture:

"If, therefore, the whole church comes together and all speak in tongues, and outsiders or unbelievers enter, will they not say that you are out of your minds? But if all prophesy, and an unbeliever or outsider enters, he is convicted by all, he is called to account by all, the secrets of his heart are disclosed, and so, falling on his face, he will worship God and declare that God is really among you." (1 Corinthians 14:23–25)

Paul paints two contrasting pictures of worship in this passage: one filled with confusion and chaos, and the other with clarity and conviction. His message to the Corinthians is clear: the faithful practice of spiritual gifts must always glorify God, edify the church, and draw people to Him.

The first scenario Paul describes is a chaotic gathering where everyone is speaking in tongues simultaneously. For an outsider or unbeliever, this scene would be bewildering. Without understanding the words or their purpose, they would likely dismiss the experience as madness. Paul's concern is not just about orderliness but about the church's witness. Worship should reflect the character of God—peaceful, purposeful, and full of truth.

Now imagine the second scenario. Instead of unintelligible speech, prophetic words are shared—words spoken in a language the outsider can understand. These words reveal the secrets of the heart, offering insight, encouragement, and conviction. The outsider is not left in confusion but is instead brought face to face with the reality of God's presence. They are moved to worship, declaring, *"God is really among you."*

Prophecy, in this context, is not about predicting the future but about speaking God's truth in a way that reveals His heart and draws people closer to Him. Paul highlights the transformative power of this gift when it is used faithfully. Prophecy makes God known and glorifies Him by touching the lives of those present in personal and profound ways.

This passage challenges us to think about the way we use spiritual gifts today. Are they exercised in ways that point people to Jesus, or do they create confusion or self-centeredness? Paul's teaching reminds us that the goal of every gift is to glorify God and build up His church. When used faithfully and in love, spiritual gifts can reveal God's presence and power in extraordinary ways.

■ *Reflection:*

Have you ever been blessed or challenged by a word of prophecy? Do you believe it is a gift that should be exercised in the church today? Reflect on Paul's encouragement to the Corinthians to seek this gift. What might God be inviting you to seek or practice in your own life?

■ *Prayer:*

Lord, thank You for the gifts You have given to Your church. Teach me to use them faithfully and with love, always seeking to glorify You and edify others. Help me to be open to Your Spirit's leading and to speak Your truth with clarity and boldness, so that others may come to know You. Amen.

Day 20: Order Leads to Edification

Scripture:

"What then, brothers? When you come together, each one has a hymn, a lesson, a revelation, a tongue, or an interpretation. Let all things be done for building up. If any speak in a tongue, let there be only two or at most three, and each in turn, and let someone interpret. But if there is no one to interpret, let each of them keep silent in church and speak to himself and to God. Let two or three prophets speak, and let the others weigh what is said. If a revelation is made to another sitting there, let the first be silent. For you can all prophesy one by one, so that all may learn and all be encouraged, and the spirits of prophets are subject to prophets." (1 Corinthians 14:26–32)

Paul's instruction to the Corinthian church centers on one overarching goal: *"Let all things be done for building up."* This is not about individual expression or personal gratification—it's about the entire body of Christ growing together in faith and unity, worshiping Jesus as Lord. The church's purpose is to glorify God and edify His people. When everything is done in order and harmony, the church reflects God's perfect design and character.

Paul envisions a church where every member contributes their gifts in a way that glorifies God and strengthens others. Hymns, lessons, revelations, tongues, and prophecies—all are welcome, but they must be exercised with care and respect for the gathered community. This requires humility, love, and a willingness to submit personal desires to the greater good of the church.

Orderliness in worship is not about suppressing the Spirit but about creating an environment where the Spirit can work effectively. Paul offers practical guidelines: only two or three should speak in tongues, and only if there is an interpreter. Similarly, two or three prophets may speak, but their words must be tested. Prophecies are weighed against Scripture and discerned by the congregation to ensure they align with God's truth. This kind of structure ensures that worship is intelligible, edifying, and centered on God, not on human performance.

Paul's instructions challenge us to evaluate our own approach to worship. Do we come to church ready to glorify God and build up others? Or do we come with personal agendas—critiquing the music, the sermon, or the behavior of others? True worship requires us to set aside selfishness and distractions, focusing instead on God and His purposes.

Imagine a church where every member comes with a heart aligned to God's will, eager to serve, worship, and encourage one another. That's the picture Paul paints—a church that reflects the love, order, and unity of heaven itself.

■ Reflection:

How might Paul's guidance shape your approach to worship? Are there areas in your heart that need to be realigned to God's purposes? Consider how you can contribute to the edification of others in your church community.

■ Prayer:

Lord, thank You for Your design for the church. Help me to approach worship with a heart focused on glorifying You and building up others. Teach me to use my gifts in humility and love, submitting to Your order and purpose. Align my heart, mind, and actions to Your perfect plan. Amen.

Day 21: Order and Peace in the Church

Scripture:

"For God is not a God of confusion but of peace. As in all the churches of the saints, the women should keep silent in the churches. For they are not permitted to speak, but should be in submission, as the Law also says. If there is anything they desire to learn, let them ask their husbands at home. For it is shameful for a woman to speak in church." (1 Corinthians 14:33–35)

Paul's words in this passage reflect his desire for the Corinthian church to honor God by worshiping in a way that reflects His nature—peaceful, orderly, and glorifying to Him. The Corinthian believers were coming out of chaotic and often immoral pagan worship practices. Their church gatherings, influenced by these old ways, were often disorderly, causing confusion rather than edification. Paul's instructions were meant to establish a new rhythm, one that mirrored the character of the one true God.

The cultural context of the time is essential to understanding Paul's words. In Corinth, pagan temples often allowed wild, ecstatic expressions of worship, with women playing prominent but often unholy roles. In the Christian church, Paul sought to ensure that worship was distinct from these practices, grounded in reverence and order.

The instruction for women to remain silent in the church assembly is one of the most debated passages in Scripture. Many scholars suggest that Paul was addressing a specific issue in the Corinthian church, perhaps related to women interrupting the service or questioning teachings during worship. This silence may have been a temporary guideline to prevent disruptions and foster learning in an orderly manner.

It is also critical to view Paul's words through the broader lens of Scripture. Jesus elevated women throughout His ministry, breaking cultural norms by teaching them, engaging with them in meaningful theological discussions, and entrusting them with critical roles, such as being the first witnesses to His resurrection. Paul himself commended women who labored alongside him in the Gospel, such as Priscilla, Phoebe, and Lydia. These examples remind us that women were and continue to be essential in the life and mission of the church.

Ultimately, Paul's message is about order and peace in worship. God is not glorified by chaos but by gatherings that reflect His character. Just as every person in the assembly—men and women alike—was called to respect and maintain order, we too are called to create worship spaces that glorify God and edify His people.

■ Reflection:

Where in your life do you need to experience God's peace? Are there areas of chaos—at home, in your mind, at work, or in your relationships—that you need to surrender to Him? Spend time in prayer today, asking God to bring His peace and order into those areas.

■ Prayer:

Lord, You are a God of peace and order, and I praise You for Your perfect nature. Help me to reflect that peace in my worship and my daily life. I surrender the chaos of my circumstances to You and ask You to breathe Your peace into every corner of my heart, mind, and relationships. Amen.

Week 4:

The Hope of the Resurrection

Day 22: People Under Authority

Scripture:

"Or was it from you that the word of God came? Or are you the only ones it has reached? If anyone thinks that he is a prophet, or spiritual, he should acknowledge that the things I am writing to you are a command of the Lord. If anyone does not recognize this, he is not recognized. So, my brothers, earnestly desire to prophesy, and do not forbid speaking in tongues. But all things should be done decently and in order." (1 Corinthians 14:36–40)

The Corinthians were enamored with their spiritual gifts, often using them in ways that drew attention to themselves rather than glorifying God. Paul, like a firm but loving parent, reminded them of an essential truth: their gifts came from God, not themselves. These gifts were not earned or deserved but given by grace, and they were to be exercised under God's authority and for His glory.

Paul's rebuke is pointed: *"Or was it from you that the word of God came?"* His words challenge any notion of self-importance. The Corinthians needed to remember their place as recipients of God's grace, not originators of it. Their gifts and spiritual experiences should lead to humility and submission, not pride or disorder.

Submission to God's authority is a fundamental mark of the Christian life. Everything—our time, resources, talents, and yes, our spiritual gifts—must be surrendered to the Lord. For the Corinthians, this meant acknowledging that the exercise of their gifts should align with God's purposes and His design for worship. Paul was clear: if someone refused to recognize God's authority as expressed in His Word, they would not be recognized within the church. Order and reverence were non-negotiable.

This call to submission is just as relevant today. In a culture that often prioritizes personal autonomy and subjective truth, Paul's reminder of God's absolute authority stands as a needed corrective. We do not get to decide what is right or true based on our feelings or circumstances. As followers of Christ, we live under the authority of His Word, which is unchanging and always true.

Submitting to God's authority can be challenging, especially when it conflicts with our desires or understanding. But when we remember that His ways are higher than ours and that His plans are always motivated by perfect love, submission becomes a joyful act of trust. God's authority is not oppressive; it is life-giving. He knows us, loves us, and desires our ultimate good.

Paul's call to the Corinthians—and to us—is to live as people under authority, recognizing that all we have comes from God and exists for His glory. This posture of submission not only honors God but also brings peace, order, and flourishing to His church.

▪ Reflection:

Are there areas of your life where you struggle to submit to God's authority? Bring those to Him in prayer, along with any doubts or questions. Ask Him to reveal any areas where you are holding back and to help you trust Him more fully.

▪ Prayer:

Lord, thank You for being a God of love, order, and authority. Teach me to submit every area of my life to You, trusting in Your perfect wisdom and care. Help me to use the gifts You've given me in ways that glorify You and build up Your church. Amen.

Day 23: Are You Being Saved by the Gospel?

Scripture:

"Now I would remind you, brothers, of the gospel I preached to you, which you received, in which you stand, and by which you are being saved, if you hold fast to the word I preached to you—unless you believed in vain." (1 Corinthians 15:1–2)

Paul, nearing the close of his letter, brings the Corinthians back to the foundation of their faith: the Gospel. He reminds them of the message they received—the truth in which they stand and by which they are being saved. But he also issues a warning: salvation requires holding fast to the truth, and drifting from it puts their faith at risk.

The Corinthians had lost clarity on a critical doctrine: the resurrection. Not only were they struggling to honor and recognize one another as members of Christ's body, but some doubted God's ultimate plan of bodily resurrection for His people. For Paul, this was a crisis of faith. If they rejected the resurrection of believers, they undermined the very Gospel they claimed to believe.

Paul takes them back to the beginning, to the Gospel message he preached when he first came to them: Jesus Christ, the Messiah, lived a sinless life, died for the sins of the world, and rose again on the third day, defeating death, sin, and Satan. Through His atoning work, all who believe are saved from sin and adopted as children of God. This Gospel is not just the foundation of faith; it is the ongoing power by which believers are being saved, transformed, and sustained.

Yet the Corinthians were at risk of abandoning this truth. Their doubts about the resurrection revealed a deeper struggle: they were still clinging to old ways of thinking and living, unwilling to fully submit to God's truth. Paul is direct: if they reject the resurrection, their faith is in vain. Without the resurrection, the Gospel loses its power and hope.

Paul reminds them—and us—that God's plan is both physical and spiritual. Just as Jesus was raised bodily from the dead, so too will His followers receive glorious, resurrected bodies when He returns. This promise is not just theological; it has practical implications. Believing in the resurrection shapes how we live now, fostering integrity and hope as members of Christ's body on earth.

The resurrection is our ultimate hope, reminding us that death is not the end. For those who trust in Christ, there is the promise of eternal life in a glorified body, free from sin, suffering, and death.

■ Reflection:

What is your view of the resurrection, and how does it shape your hope? Are you holding fast to the Gospel, or are there areas where doubt has crept in? Reflect on the glory of the resurrected body and the eternal life that awaits those who trust in Jesus.

■ Prayer:

Lord, thank You for the Gospel, the foundation of my faith and the source of my hope. Help me to hold fast to Your truth and live with clarity and commitment to the promise of the resurrection. Strengthen my faith, and keep my heart set on the glory that awaits in Your eternal kingdom. Amen.

Day 24: The Things of First Importance

Scripture:

"For I delivered to you as of first importance what I also received: that Christ died for our sins in accordance with the Scriptures, that he was buried, that he was raised on the third day in accordance with the Scriptures, and that he appeared to Cephas, then to the twelve. Then he appeared to more than five hundred brothers at one time, most of whom are still alive, though some have fallen asleep. Then he appeared to James, then to all the apostles. Last of all, as to one untimely born, he appeared also to me." (1 Corinthians 15:3–8)

Sometimes we make things more complicated than they need to be. Whether it's overthinking a recipe or adding unnecessary steps to a simple task, we often end up frustrated and overwhelmed. The Corinthians had fallen into a similar trap with their faith, overcomplicating the Gospel with their own ideas and preferences. Paul's response was clear: go back to the basics.

Paul reminds the Corinthians of the core truths of Christianity—what he calls the things of *first importance*. These foundational truths are simple, yet they hold the weight of eternity:

1. **Christ died for our sins** in accordance with the Scriptures.
2. **He was buried,** confirming His death was real.
3. **He was raised on the third day,** also in accordance with the Scriptures.
4. **He appeared** to many, providing undeniable proof of His resurrection.

This is the Gospel in its purest form. Paul emphasizes that these truths are not just ideas or beliefs; they are historical realities, witnessed by many. Jesus' resurrection was not a myth or metaphor. He appeared to Peter, the disciples, over 500 followers, James, the apostles, and finally to Paul himself. Each of these encounters transformed lives and became the foundation for the early church.

James' story is particularly powerful. As Jesus' brother, James had grown up with Him but did not believe He was the Messiah. Yet after encountering the risen Jesus, James' life was radically changed. He became a devoted leader of the church and gave his life to proclaiming the Gospel. This transformation highlights the undeniable power of the resurrection.

Paul's message is timeless. In a world that often complicates faith with personal preferences, cultural trends, or intellectual debates, the Gospel remains simple and unchanging. These truths—Christ's death, burial, resurrection, and appearances—are the foundation on which the church stands. They are the bedrock of our faith, hope, and salvation.

If you find yourself overwhelmed or confused in your spiritual life, Paul's words invite you to return to the basics. Remember what Christ has done for you, trust in the power of His resurrection, and let these foundational truths shape your faith and your life.

■ Reflection:

Are there areas in your faith where you've added unnecessary complications or lost sight of the essentials? Take time today to reflect on the things of first importance and how they bring clarity, hope, and focus to your walk with Christ.

■ Prayer:

Lord, thank You for the simple yet profound truths of the Gospel. Help me to hold fast to the things of first importance and to build my life on the foundation of Christ's death, burial, and resurrection. Renew my faith and my hope as I remember all You have done for me. Amen.

Day 25: The Transformative Grace of God

Scripture:

"For I am the least of the apostles, unworthy to be called an apostle, because I persecuted the church of God. But by the grace of God I am what I am, and his grace toward me was not in vain. On the contrary, I worked harder than any of them, though it was not I, but the grace of God that is with me. Whether then it was I or they, so we preach and so you believed." (1 Corinthians 15:9–11)

Paul's relationship with the Corinthian church was complicated. Despite being their spiritual father—planting the church and guiding them in the faith—the Corinthians were often critical of him. They judged his physical appearance, dismissed his humility, and even questioned his spirituality. In their arrogance, they elevated themselves, believing they were more spiritual than the man who had introduced them to Christ.

How did Paul respond to such arrogance? Not with pride or a list of his accomplishments, but with a profound humility rooted in the grace of God. He openly acknowledged his past as a persecutor of the church, calling himself *"the least of the apostles."* By human standards, Paul was unworthy of his calling. But Paul knew that his life was not about what he deserved—it was about God's grace.

Paul's story is a testament to the transformative power of grace. On the road to Damascus, Jesus met Paul in the midst of his sin and rebellion. That encounter changed everything. Grace not only forgave Paul's sins but also empowered him to become one of the greatest missionaries in history. As Paul himself said, *"By the grace of God I am what I am."*

This grace didn't make Paul complacent; it fueled his work for the Lord. Paul labored tirelessly to preach the Gospel, establish churches, and disciple believers. Yet even in his hard work, Paul recognized that it was not his own strength but God's grace working through him. His life was a living testimony to the power of God's unmerited favor.

Paul's message to the Corinthians—and to us—is clear: everything we are and everything we do for God is by His grace. There is no room for pride, arrogance, or self-reliance. Just as Paul needed grace, so do we. We are all sinners saved by grace, called to live lives that reflect the transformative power of Christ's love.

■ *Reflection:*

Have you embraced the truth that you are saved by grace alone? Are there areas in your life where pride or self-reliance have crept in? Take time today to reflect on the transformative grace of God and how it empowers you to live for Him.

■ *Prayer:*

Lord, thank You for Your amazing grace that saves, transforms, and empowers me. Help me to live in humility, recognizing that all I am and all I do is by Your grace. Teach me to extend that same grace to others, reflecting Your love and mercy in my life. Amen.

Day 26: Is Your Faith in Vain?

Scripture:

"Now if Christ is proclaimed as raised from the dead, how can some of you say that there is no resurrection of the dead? But if there is no resurrection of the dead, then not even Christ has been raised. And if Christ has not been raised, then our preaching is in vain and your faith is in vain. We are even found to be misrepresenting God, because we testified about God that he raised Christ, whom he did not raise if it is true that the dead are not raised."
(1 Corinthians 15:12–15)

Paul addresses the Corinthians with an argument that is as sharp as it is logical: If there is no resurrection, then Christ has not been raised. If Christ has not been raised, the entire Christian faith crumbles. The resurrection of Jesus is not just a detail of the Gospel—it is its very foundation.

The Corinthians, despite their newfound faith, were adopting ideas that denied the resurrection of the dead. Influenced by cultural and philosophical assumptions, they claimed to believe in Christ while rejecting the resurrection. Paul's response cuts straight to the heart of their error: Denying the resurrection denies the very truth that brings salvation.

Paul reminds them of the eyewitnesses: the disciples, James, the apostles, and over 500 others who saw the risen Christ. These were not abstract claims but concrete testimonies of real people who encountered Jesus after His death. Paul himself, once a zealous persecutor of the church, was transformed by the risen Lord on the road to Damascus. Would all these witnesses fabricate a lie?

But more importantly, Paul points out the spiritual implications. If Christ has not been raised, then faith is futile. The Gospel becomes meaningless, Christian teaching becomes a lie, and humanity remains trapped in sin and death. The resurrection is not just proof of Jesus' divinity—it is the demonstration of God's victory over sin, death, and the grave. Without it, there is no hope, no forgiveness, no salvation.

Paul's words to the Corinthians are just as relevant today. In a world where people often seek to reinterpret or diminish the resurrection as metaphorical or unnecessary, the truth of the Gospel remains clear: Jesus rose bodily from the dead. This truth is the foundation of our faith and the source of our hope. To deny it is to deny the very essence of Christianity.

■ Reflection:

The resurrection is central to the Gospel. Do you believe in the physical resurrection of Jesus Christ? How does this truth shape your faith and your hope for the future? Reflect on the witnesses, the Scriptures, and your own faith journey as you answer this most important question.

■ Prayer:

Lord, thank You for the hope of the resurrection. I believe that Jesus died for my sins and rose again on the third day. Strengthen my faith in this truth and help me to live in the hope and power of Your victory over sin and death. Amen.

Day 27: The People Who Are to Be Most Pitied

Scripture:

"For if the dead are not raised, not even Christ has been raised. And if Christ has not been raised, your faith is futile and you are still in your sins. Then those also who have fallen asleep in Christ have perished. If in Christ we have hope in this life only, we are of all people most to be pitied." (1 Corinthians 15:16–19)

Paul's words here are stark and sobering. He forces the Corinthians—and us—to grapple with the implications of denying the resurrection. If there is no resurrection, then Christ Himself has not been raised. If Christ has not been raised, the entire Christian faith collapses.

The resurrection of Jesus is not an optional belief or a secondary doctrine; it is the cornerstone of Christianity. Without it, our faith is meaningless, and humanity remains trapped in sin and death. For Paul, this truth is so central that if it were not true, Christians would be the most pitiable people in the world. Why? Because they have devoted their lives to a false hope, sacrificing worldly pleasures and enduring persecution for something that isn't real.

Imagine living as a Christian without the hope of the resurrection. Without the promise of eternal life, the sacrifices we make—renouncing sin, suffering for Christ, living for others—would seem foolish. Without the resurrection, those who have died in Christ have simply perished, and there is no comfort for the grieving or hope for the future. This is the grim conclusion of a resurrection-less Gospel.

Paul's argument challenges the Corinthians' faulty logic and prideful assertions. They had embraced a worldview that denied the resurrection while still trying to claim the benefits of faith in Christ. But as Paul shows, you cannot separate the resurrection from the Gospel. To do so is to undermine everything that Christianity stands for.

The same challenge applies to us today. In a culture that often wants to reinterpret or minimize core Christian beliefs, it's tempting to compromise on doctrines like the resurrection to make the faith more palatable. But Paul reminds us that the resurrection is non-negotiable. Without it, there is no forgiveness, no freedom, and no future.

Thankfully, Paul doesn't stop at this grim conclusion. He will go on to declare the glorious truth that Christ *has* been raised from the dead, ensuring hope, redemption, and eternal life for all who believe. For now, his words challenge us to examine our faith, confront doubts, and reaffirm the centrality of the resurrection in our lives.

■ Reflection:

Where do you see similar faulty logic in the world today? Are there core beliefs of Christianity that you've been tempted to compromise? Reflect on Paul's words and consider how the resurrection shapes your faith, hope, and daily life.

■ Prayer:

Lord, thank You for the hope of the resurrection. Help me to stand firm in this truth, even when the world denies it or I face doubts. Strengthen my faith, and let my life reflect the hope and joy of Your victory over sin and death. Amen.

Day 28: The Victory of Jesus!

Scripture:

"But in fact Christ has been raised from the dead, the firstfruits of those who have fallen asleep. For as by a man came death, by a man has come also the resurrection of the dead. For as in Adam all die, so also in Christ shall all be made alive. But each in his own order: Christ the firstfruits, then at his coming those who belong to Christ. Then comes the end, when he delivers the kingdom to God the Father after destroying every rule and every authority and power. For he must reign until he has put all his enemies under his feet." (1 Corinthians 15:20–25)

At this point in his letter, Paul stops entertaining the Corinthians' doubts and faulty logic. Instead, he boldly declares the truth of the Gospel: *"Christ has been raised from the dead"* (v. 20). Though the Corinthians had been wrong in their beliefs about the resurrection, being corrected brought them an incredible benefit—true hope in the promise of resurrection for all believers.

One of the few certainties in this life is death. You will die. I will die. Everyone will die, except those who remain alive at the second coming of Jesus Christ. For the rest of us, death is unavoidable. But because of Jesus' resurrection, death is not the end for those who trust in Him. Like Jesus, you will be made alive. You will receive a resurrected body—perfect, whole, fully restored, and redeemed. No more sickness, no more pain, and no more striving. Yes, that means no more dieting or hard workouts in the gym. Even better, you will live forever in the glory of Jesus Christ.

This hope is more than wishful thinking; it is a promise guaranteed by God. Paul refers to Jesus as the *firstfruits*—the first of the harvest and a pledge of what is to come. Jesus' resurrection is God's assurance that what He did for Jesus, He will also do for you. Through Jesus, you will conquer death and experience the joy of eternal life.

As a believer, you are part of Christ's victory. Not only will you share in His glory, but you will also share in His triumph. Before ascending to heaven, Jesus promised to return and fully establish His kingdom. On that day, all sin, death, and evil will be destroyed. Every earthly power and authority will fall, and Jesus will reign forever as King. In His kingdom, there will be no more tears, no more pain, and no more darkness. What a glorious day that will be!

■ *Reflection:*

Have you, like the Corinthians, ever experienced the joy of being wrong and discovering a greater truth? Why is it so important to remain humble and teachable, especially in matters of faith? Are there areas where God is calling you to embrace humility today?

■ *Prayer:*

Lord Jesus, thank You for the victory of Your resurrection. Help me to stand firm in the hope and promise of eternal life with You. Teach me to be humble and open to Your truth, even when it challenges my understanding. Let my life reflect the joy of Your coming kingdom. Amen.

Week 5:

The Glory of the Resurrection

Day 29: Godly Humility and Hope

Scripture:

"The last enemy to be destroyed is death. For 'God has put all things in subjection under his feet.' But when it says, 'all things are put in subjection,' it is plain that he is excepted who put all things in subjection under him. When all things are subjected to him, then the Son himself will also be subjected to him who put all things in subjection under him, that God may be all in all."
(1 Corinthians 15:26–28)

No one escapes the sting of death. By the time I was 22, I had experienced the death of three high school friends, my best friend's mother, my grandparents, and, most devastatingly, one of my closest friends in college. Many of these losses were sudden and heartbreaking, leaving holes in my heart and in the hearts of those who loved them.

At her funeral, my college friend was remembered with a quote she had shared: *"Christians never say goodbye, just see you later."* Those words became a lifeline for me, a reminder that in Christ, death is not the end. One day, I will see her again—not just for a fleeting moment but in the fullness of eternal life with God.

Paul acknowledges the pain of death but also offers hope: death itself will one day be destroyed. Through His death and resurrection, Jesus broke the power of death. As the song "Glorious Day" by Casting Crowns proclaims, *"Death could not hold Him, the grave could not keep Him from rising again."* Jesus' resurrection is not just His victory—it is our guarantee.

Yet, we still live in the tension of the *now, but not yet*. Death remains a part of our earthly reality. We grieve the loss of loved ones, and we wrestle with the brokenness of this world. But as believers, we grieve with hope. We hold onto the promise that Jesus will return to fully establish His kingdom, where death, sin, and pain will be no more.

Paul assures the Corinthians that this hope is not in vain. God's ultimate plan will come to fruition: all things will be subjected to Christ, and Christ Himself will submit to the Father, bringing everything under God's reign. *"God will be all in all"*—a picture of perfect unity, peace, and restoration.

This promise invites us to trust in God's sovereignty and timing. Even as we groan and wait for the fulfillment of His kingdom, we can rest in the assurance that death's days are numbered, and life eternal awaits.

■ Reflection:

How does this passage bring hope to your heart today? In Christ, pain, sin, and death are temporary, and eternal life is guaranteed. Reflect on how this truth transforms the way you grieve, hope, and live each day.

■ Prayer:

Lord, thank You for the promise that death will be destroyed and that eternal life with You is certain. Comfort me in the midst of grief and give me the strength to wait with hope for Your kingdom to come. Teach me to trust in Your timing and to live each day in light of Your eternal victory. Amen.

Day 30: How Do We Live in the Now but Not Yet?

Scripture:

"Otherwise, what do people mean by being baptized on behalf of the dead? If the dead are not raised at all, why are people baptized on their behalf? Why are we in danger every hour? I protest, brothers, by my pride in you, which I have in Christ Jesus our Lord, I die every day! What do I gain if, humanly speaking, I fought with beasts at Ephesus? If the dead are not raised, 'Let us eat and drink, for tomorrow we die.' Do not be deceived: 'Bad company ruins good morals.' Wake up from your drunken stupor, as is right, and do not go on sinning. For some have no knowledge of God. I say this to your shame." (1 Corinthians 15:29–34)

Paul refuses to let up on the Corinthians' misunderstandings because the stakes are too high. Their flawed theology about the resurrection wasn't just an intellectual issue—it jeopardized their faith, their hope, and their salvation. With rhetorical questions and hard truths, Paul confronts their inconsistency and challenges them to live in light of the Gospel.

The Corinthians revered baptism, which Paul affirmed as a powerful sign of salvation: dying with Christ, rising to new life, and receiving the promise of eternity. Yet their actions betrayed their beliefs. Some even practiced a strange custom of being baptized on behalf of the dead, despite denying the resurrection of the dead. Paul exposes the futility of their logic: why uphold baptism if there's no resurrection? Why cling to practices pointing to eternal life if they didn't believe in it?

Paul then turns the lens on himself. His life was marked by sacrifice and danger—risking death daily to preach the Gospel, endure persecution, and build the church. If the resurrection wasn't real, why would he bother? Without the hope of eternal life, everything—faith, sacrifice, even suffering—becomes meaningless. The alternative would be to embrace the empty mantra: *"Let us eat and drink, for tomorrow we die."*

But Paul doesn't stop at exposing their errors. He calls them to action with urgency: *"Wake up from your drunken stupor, as is right, and do not go on sinning."* Their denial of the resurrection and their worldly conduct betrayed a lack of knowledge of God. They were living as if God didn't exist, and Paul warns them—and us—not to fall into that trap.

For believers, the *now but not yet* reality of God's kingdom shapes how we live. We live in a fallen world but as redeemed people. We know the promise of eternal life and await the day when Christ will establish His kingdom in full. While we wait, we're called to live in hope, pursue holiness, and grow in the knowledge of God.

■ *Reflection:*

How are you doing in the waiting? Are there areas of your life where you've grown complacent or fallen into worldly patterns? Do you need Paul's wake-up call: *"Wake up, stop sinning, and live in the knowledge of God"*? Take time to reflect on how you can live more fully in light of the Gospel today.

■ *Prayer:*

Lord, thank You for the promise of resurrection and the hope of eternal life. Help me to wake up, turn from sin, and live in the knowledge of Your truth. Teach me to live as one redeemed, waiting faithfully for the fulfillment of Your kingdom. Amen.

Day 31: The Hope of a Resurrected Body

Scripture:

"But someone will ask, 'How are the dead raised? With what kind of body do they come?' You foolish person! What you sow does not come to life unless it dies. And what you sow is not the body that is to be, but a bare kernel, perhaps of wheat or of some other grain. But God gives it a body as he has chosen, and to each kind of seed its own body." (1 Corinthians 15:35–38)

Sometimes those who consider themselves the wisest among us are, in fact, the most foolish. Paul confronted such prideful foolishness among the Corinthians as they struggled to comprehend the resurrection. Through an imaginary dialogue, Paul tackled their skepticism head-on, addressing both their questions and their objections.

The Corinthians could not understand how God could raise the dead or what kind of body they would have. So, instead of trusting God's promises, they dismissed the resurrection altogether. Paul exposed the arrogance of this reasoning with a sharp rebuke: *"You foolish person!"* Their problem wasn't just intellectual—it was spiritual. They relied on worldly wisdom and human understanding instead of humbly submitting to God's Word.

True wisdom, as Proverbs reminds us, begins with *"the fear of the Lord"* (Proverbs 9:10). It requires humility, reverence, and a willingness to acknowledge that God's ways are higher than ours. The Corinthians' skepticism revealed their lack of this wisdom.

They assumed that if they couldn't understand something, it must not be true.

To illustrate the resurrection, Paul used the analogy of a seed. A seed must die before it can bring forth new life. What is sown in the ground is not the same as what grows—it is transformed into something greater. In the same way, our earthly bodies will be sown in death but raised in glory. God, in His infinite wisdom and power, will give each person a new, resurrected body according to His perfect design.

This promise of transformation is not just a theological idea—it is a source of profound hope. Paul later described this hope to the Philippians: *"Our citizenship is in heaven, and from it we await a Savior, the Lord Jesus Christ, who will transform our lowly body to be like his glorious body"* (Philippians 3:20–21). In Christ, death is not the end. It is the gateway to a new, eternal life with a glorious, resurrected body.

■ *Reflection:*

Do you trust in God's promise of a resurrected body, even when it surpasses your understanding? Or do you struggle with the temptation to rely on worldly wisdom instead of God's Word? Spend time meditating on Proverbs 9:10 today, asking the Lord to grant you His wisdom and strengthen your hope in His promises.

■ *Prayer:*

Lord, thank You for the promise of a glorious, resurrected body. Help me to trust in Your wisdom and to humbly submit to Your Word, even when I don't fully understand. Teach me to embrace the hope of the resurrection and to live in light of eternity. Amen.

Day 32: A Future Glory for You

Scripture:

"For not all flesh is the same, but there is one kind for humans, another for animals, another for birds, and another for fish. There are heavenly bodies and earthly bodies, but the glory of the heavenly is of one kind, and the glory of the earthly is of another. There is one glory of the sun, and another glory of the moon, and another glory of the stars; for star differs from star in glory."
(1 Corinthians 15:39–41)

You are made in the image of God, and as His redeemed child, you reflect His glory in this world. Even in your earthly body, there is inherent glory, but an even greater glory awaits you. Pause for a moment and reflect on this incredible truth: you are the temple of the living God (1 Corinthians 3:16). His glory dwells within you and shines through you. The deep yearning for glory within your soul is not misplaced—it is part of how God created you. You were made for glory.

In today's passage, Paul continues his exploration of the promise of the resurrection by pointing to the diversity of God's creation and the various degrees of glory within it. He notes the different kinds of glory among humans, animals, birds, and fish. Similarly, the heavenly bodies—such as the sun, moon, and stars—each have their own unique splendor. Paul uses this as a metaphor to help us understand the distinction between our earthly bodies and the heavenly, resurrected bodies we will receive.

While our current bodies reflect God's glory, they are merely a shadow of what is to come. The glory of our earthly bodies pales in comparison to the glory of the resurrected body that awaits us. In *Mere Christianity*, C.S. Lewis captures this longing beautifully: *"If I find in myself a desire which no experience in this world can satisfy, the most probable explanation is that I was made for another world."* This longing points us forward, reminding us that we are destined for something far greater.

Your resurrected body will be fully renewed, perfectly reflecting God's glory. It's not just your physical body that will be restored—your heart, mind, and spirit will also be made whole. You will be complete. This future glory is not simply a theological concept but a source of hope and joy that can shape how you live today.

God invites you to lean into this hope, to let it stir your heart and motivate you to live faithfully now. While we enjoy glimpses of God's glory in this life, they are only a foretaste of the fullness that awaits.

■ Reflection:

Have you considered how your deepest longings point to the glory that awaits you? What does the Lord want you to anticipate about your future glory? How can this hope equip you to live with greater faithfulness and joy in your current body today?

■ Prayer:

Lord, thank You for creating me in Your image and filling me with Your glory. Help me to live in anticipation of the future glory that awaits me. Teach me to reflect Your glory now and to live with hope, joy, and faithfulness as I wait for the fullness of Your promises. Amen.

Day 33: The Glory That Awaits You

Scripture:

"So is it with the resurrection of the dead. What is sown is perishable; what is raised is imperishable. It is sown in dishonor; it is raised in glory. It is sown in weakness; it is raised in power. It is sown a natural body; it is raised a spiritual body. If there is a natural body, there is also a spiritual body."
(1 Corinthians 15:42–44)

Paul continues to explore the resurrection with striking contrasts between our current physical bodies and the resurrected bodies we will receive. These distinctions would have been surprising to his original audience in Corinth and remain thought-provoking for us today.

In modern culture, we place enormous emphasis on physical appearance and fitness. The diet and beauty industries thrive on our obsession with how we look and feel. From gym memberships to cosmetic surgeries, people invest significant time, money, and energy into improving and preserving their physical bodies. While caring for our health is important, Paul encourages us to shift our perspective from the temporal to the eternal.

Paul contrasts the characteristics of our earthly bodies with those of our future resurrected bodies:

- **Perishable vs. Imperishable:** Our current bodies age, decay, and ultimately die. Our resurrected bodies, however, will never deteriorate or face death.

- **Dishonor vs. Glory:** While our earthly bodies bear the marks of sin and brokenness, our resurrected bodies will reflect the fullness of God's glory.

- **Weakness vs. Power:** The physical limitations we experience now—sickness, fatigue, and frailty—will be replaced with perfect strength and vitality.
- **Natural vs. Spiritual:** Our present bodies are tied to this earthly existence, but our resurrected bodies will be fully attuned to the spiritual realities of God's eternal kingdom.

Paul assures us that the best is yet to come. These earthly bodies, though marvelous in their design, are temporary. The resurrected bodies we will receive are eternal, glorious, and powerful—like the body of Jesus after His resurrection. Every struggle, pain, or limitation you face now will be completely obliterated. In its place will be perfect restoration and everlasting life.

This promise reminds us to be good stewards of our bodies, using them for God's purposes, but not to obsess over them. Our focus should be on what is eternal, not what is fleeting. We can celebrate the beauty of our earthly existence while eagerly anticipating the glory that is to come.

▪ Reflection:

How do Paul's words challenge or encourage your perspective on your physical body? Take time to meditate on the glory that awaits you—freedom from pain, decay, and death—and the joy of living in a perfect, resurrected body.

▪ Prayer:

Lord, thank You for the promise of a glorious, resurrected body. Help me to be a good steward of my earthly body while keeping my focus on the eternal hope You have given me. Fill me with the joy and anticipation of the perfection and glory that await in Your presence. Amen.

Day 34: A Mystery Revealed

Scripture:

"Thus it is written, 'The first man Adam became a living being'; the last Adam became a life-giving spirit. But it is not the spiritual that is first but the natural, and then the spiritual. The first man was from the earth, a man of dust; the second man is from heaven. As was the man of dust, so also are those who are of the dust, and as is the man of heaven, so also are those who are of heaven. Just as we have borne the image of the man of dust, we shall also bear the image of the man of heaven. I tell you this, brothers: flesh and blood cannot inherit the kingdom of God, nor does the perishable inherit the imperishable. Behold! I tell you a mystery. We shall not all sleep, but we shall all be changed, in a moment, in the twinkling of an eye, at the last trumpet. For the trumpet will sound, and the dead will be raised imperishable, and we shall be changed. For this perishable body must put on the imperishable, and this mortal body must put on immortality." (1 Corinthians 15:45–53)

Right now, you bear the image of Adam, the first man created from dust. Your life exists because of the breath of God, but like Adam, your earthly body is destined to return to dust. This is the reality of all humanity. Yet in this passage, Paul reveals a divine mystery—a truth once hidden but now unveiled through Jesus' resurrection.

What is this mystery? While all people share Adam's earthly nature, not everyone will experience death as Adam did. When Jesus returns, those alive at His coming will not face physical death but will be transformed. In an instant, at the sound of the last trumpet, their perishable, mortal bodies will be changed into imperishable, immortal ones. This transformation is necessary because no one can enter God's kingdom in a natural body. His glory would overwhelm and consume us.

This mystery fills us with hope and anticipation. The trumpet will sound, signaling the moment when God's plan reaches its culmination. Whether we are among the living or the dead, we will all be changed, clothed in imperishable glory.

But how do we live in preparation for that day? Paul encourages us to view our lives now as a rehearsal for eternity. By cultivating the fruit of the Spirit—love, joy, peace, patience, kindness, goodness, faithfulness, gentleness, and self-control (Galatians 5:22–23)—we practice the godliness that will define our resurrected lives.

Even the spiritual gifts, which Paul discusses throughout this letter, serve as a foretaste of what is to come. These glimpses of God's supernatural work in and through us remind us of the transformation we will experience when we see Him face to face.

The resurrection of Jesus has revealed both the mystery of what we will become and the plan for how it will happen. Each day, we are invited to participate in the ongoing transformation God is working in us, knowing that the best is yet to come.

■ Reflection:

Do you think about the second coming of Jesus Christ? How are you preparing yourself for that day? You could be part of the revealed mystery—those who never taste physical death but are transformed in an instant to eternal glory.

■ Prayer:

Lord, thank You for revealing the mystery of the resurrection and the promise of transformation. Help me to live each day in preparation for Your return, cultivating the fruit of the Spirit and growing in Your grace. Fill me with hope as I await the day when I will be changed to share in Your eternal glory. Amen.

Day 35: You Have Victory Through Jesus Christ

Scripture:

"When the perishable puts on the imperishable, and the mortal puts on immortality, then shall come to pass the saying that is written: 'Death is swallowed up in victory.' 'O death, where is your victory? O death, where is your sting?' The sting of death is sin, and the power of sin is the law. But thanks be to God, who gives us the victory through our Lord Jesus Christ. Therefore, my beloved brothers, be steadfast, immovable, always abounding in the work of the Lord, knowing that in the Lord your labor is not in vain." (1 Corinthians 15:54–58)

What is humanity's greatest fear? Death. It's the inevitability we all face, either contemplating our own mortality or the loss of those we love. But Paul boldly declares the greatest news ever: death has been defeated, swallowed up in victory through the resurrection of Jesus Christ. For believers, the fear of death loses its power because Christ has overcome it.

Through Jesus' death on the cross and His resurrection on the third day, He conquered sin, death, and Satan. This victory is not just His—it belongs to all who trust in Him. Though we still experience the pain and reality of death in this world, it no longer has the final say.

So, how do we live in light of this truth? Paul gives us three key instructions:

1. **Be Steadfast and Immovable:** When fear or doubt creeps in, bring it to Jesus. Pray, "Jesus, help me to know, believe, and

cling to Your truth." Root yourself in the assurance of His victory and let His promises anchor your soul.

2. **Abound in the Work of the Lord:** Our victory comes through Jesus, not our own efforts. But as recipients of His grace, we are called to live out that victory by serving God and others. This is not about earning His favor but about responding to His love and sharing it with the world.

3. **Remember Your Labor Is Not in Vain:** Everything you do for God—whether it's sharing His love, serving His people, or simply trusting in Him—is meaningful. It's part of building His kingdom, and it will be rewarded in the age to come.

Paul's message is clear: we are already victors because of Jesus. This doesn't mean life will be free from challenges or pain, but it does mean that our ultimate hope is secure. Death, sin, and Satan are defeated, and one day, we will experience that victory fully when we stand face to face with our Savior.

■ *Reflection:*

What fears do you need to bring to Jesus today? How does the promise of victory through Christ encourage you? Take time to reflect on the hope and assurance He offers and consider how you can abound in His work, trusting that your labor is never in vain.

■ *Prayer:*

Lord, thank You for the victory You have won over sin, death, and Satan. Help me to live as a victor, steadfast in faith and immovable in hope. Strengthen me to abound in Your work, knowing that my labor is not in vain. Calm my fears and fill me with the assurance of Your promises. Amen.

Week 6:

Living as the Body of Christ

Day 36: The Lord's Day

Scripture:

"Now concerning the collection for the saints: as I directed the churches of Galatia, so you also are to do. On the first day of every week, each of you is to put something aside and store it up, as he may prosper, so that there will be no collecting when I come. And when I arrive, I will send those whom you accredit by letter to carry your gift to Jerusalem. If it seems advisable that I should go also, they will accompany me." (1 Corinthians 16:1–4)

As Paul concludes his letter to the Corinthians, he offers practical instructions for their gatherings and their worship. He emphasizes two key elements: when they are to meet and what they are to do when they come together.

Paul affirms the early Christian practice of meeting on *"the first day of every week"*—Sunday, the day of Jesus' resurrection. From the earliest days of the Church, Christians have gathered on this day to worship the risen Lord, to lift their hearts together in prayer and praise, and to strengthen one another in faith.

In our modern, secularized world, the significance of the Lord's Day has been diminished. Sports practices, work schedules, exhaustion, and even the convenience of online worship often take priority over gathering in person with God's people. While these activities are not inherently wrong, they can subtly shift our focus away from the worship of God and the communal life of the Church. Paul's words remind us to pause and consider the value we place on the Lord's Day and the priorities of our hearts.

Corporate worship is more than a tradition—it is a sacred rhythm established by God. From the Old Testament Sabbath to the Church's celebration of the Lord's Day, God's people have been called to set aside time to gather, worship, and bring offerings of gratitude. Paul instructed the Corinthians to prepare their financial gifts in advance, giving generously according to their prosperity, to support the persecuted Christians in Jerusalem.

This practice of giving is not just about meeting financial needs; it is an act of worship, an expression of trust, and a way to participate in God's mission. When we give, we reflect God's generosity and invest in the growth and flourishing of His Church.

Paul's instructions are simple but profound: gather to worship, encourage one another, and contribute to the needs of the larger Church. These practices remain vital for us today.

■ Reflection:

How is your heart regarding the Lord's Day? Do you prioritize gathering with God's people for worship, or have other commitments taken precedence? What might God want to say to you about your participation in corporate worship and your offerings?

■ Prayer:

Lord, thank You for the gift of the Lord's Day, a time to gather with Your people and worship You. Help me to prioritize this sacred time, to come with a heart of gratitude, and to give generously to support Your Church. Teach me to honor You with my time, resources, and devotion. Amen.

Day 37: Is There Adversity in Fruitful Ministry?

Scripture:

"I will visit you after passing through Macedonia, for I intend to pass through Macedonia, and perhaps I will stay with you or even spend the winter, so that you may help me on my journey, wherever I go. For I do not want to see you now just in passing. I hope to spend some time with you, if the Lord permits. But I will stay in Ephesus until Pentecost, for a wide door for effective work has opened to me, and there are many adversaries."
(1 Corinthians 16:5–8)

This passage provides a fascinating glimpse into Paul's mindset as he balanced the opportunities and challenges of ministry. Paul longed to visit the Corinthians, but his plans were delayed because of a powerful opportunity for ministry in Ephesus. Surprisingly, he noted that this open door was accompanied by *"many adversaries."*

For Paul, opposition wasn't a sign to retreat; it was an expected part of fruitful ministry. This perspective challenges our modern assumptions. Many of us, especially in comfortable environments, might interpret adversity as a sign that we're in the wrong place or that God isn't blessing our efforts. Paul's example teaches us that opposition is not necessarily a sign of failure—it may even confirm that we are walking in God's will.

Jesus Himself is the ultimate example of fruitful ministry in the face of adversity. As the Son of God, He came into the world He created, yet He faced rejection, hostility, and ultimately crucifixion.

If Jesus experienced opposition, we can certainly expect to face it as well when we faithfully follow Him.

Paul's resolve came from his trust in God's sovereignty and his reliance on the Holy Spirit. He saw both the opportunity and the opposition in Ephesus as part of God's plan. He didn't avoid challenges but persevered through them, knowing that his efforts would bear fruit for the kingdom.

You, too, have a calling. God has given you unique gifts to exercise for His glory and the growth of the body of Christ. Yet, as you step into your calling, opposition may come. It's important to remember that this is not a reason to give up but an invitation to rely more fully on God's strength.

Through the Holy Spirit, you can overcome adversity just as Paul did—and just as Jesus did. Trust that God is with you, even in the challenges, and that He will use your perseverance to accomplish His purposes.

▪ Reflection:

How do you respond to adversaries or challenges in your life and ministry? Do you tend to retreat or lean into God's strength? Spend time with the Lord, asking Him to give you His perspective on opposition and to grow you in perseverance through His Holy Spirit.

▪ Prayer:

Lord, thank You for the example of Paul and his faithfulness in the face of adversity. Help me to see opposition not as a deterrent but as an opportunity to trust You more deeply. Strengthen me through Your Holy Spirit to persevere and remain faithful to Your calling. Amen.

Day 38: Let All That You Do Be Done in Love

Scripture:

"When Timothy comes, see that you put him at ease among you, for he is doing the work of the Lord, as I am. So let no one despise him. Help him on his way in peace, that he may return to me, for I am expecting him with the brothers. Now concerning our brother Apollos, I strongly urged him to visit you with the other brothers, but it was not at all his will to come now. He will come when he has opportunity. Be watchful, stand firm in the faith, act like men, be strong. Let all that you do be done in love."
(1 Corinthians 16:10–14)

As Paul concluded his letter to the Corinthians, he addressed practical matters with remarkable care and tenderness. He planned to send Timothy, his spiritual son and trusted co-laborer, to minister among them. Knowing Timothy's youth and gentleness, Paul urged the Corinthians to treat him with respect and to provide him with peace and encouragement for the journey ahead.

Paul also mentioned Apollos, another leader whose role in the Corinthian church had caused some confusion. Earlier in the letter, Paul reminded the Corinthians that their focus should not be on human leaders like himself or Apollos, but on God, who brings growth (1 Corinthians 3:6–7). Here, Paul demonstrated humility and grace, encouraging Apollos to visit the Corinthians but respecting Apollos's discernment to delay his return.

What stands out is Paul's attitude. There's no defensiveness, no rivalry, no bitterness—only a spirit of love. Whether addressing

Timothy's youth or Apollos's absence, Paul modeled how to interact with others in a way that builds up the body of Christ.

Paul then pivoted to broader instructions, exhorting the Corinthians to be watchful, stand firm in their faith, be courageous, and act with strength. Yet he didn't stop there. He added the central command: *"Let all that you do be done in love"* (v. 14).

Love is the defining mark of Christian living. Paul reminded the Corinthians that everything they do—how they treat young leaders like Timothy, how they speak about others like Apollos, and how they stand firm in their faith—must flow from love. This is the love Paul described in 1 Corinthians 13: patient, kind, humble, and selfless.

How transformative would our churches and relationships be if we applied this principle? How would our conversations, disagreements, and everyday interactions change if love were the measure of our words, actions, and thoughts?

■ *Reflection:*

Take a moment to reflect on Paul's words: *"Let all that you do be done in love."* What would it look like for this to guide your speech, your actions, and even your thoughts today? How might it transform your relationships within your family, workplace, or church?

■ *Prayer:*

Lord, thank You for the example of Paul, who showed love and humility in his dealings with others. Help me to follow his example and make love the guiding principle in all I do. Teach me to speak, act, and think in ways that glorify You and build up others. Amen.

Day 39: How to Wait Upon the Lord

Scripture:

"Now I urge you, brothers—you know that the household of Stephanas were the first converts in Achaia, and that they have devoted themselves to the service of the saints—be subject to such as these, and to every fellow worker and laborer. I rejoice at the coming of Stephanas and Fortunatus and Achaicus, because they have made up for your absence, for they refreshed my spirit as well as yours. Give recognition to such people. The churches of Asia send you greetings. Aquila and Prisca, together with the church in their house, send you hearty greetings in the Lord. All the brothers send you greetings. Greet one another with a holy kiss. I, Paul, write this greeting with my own hand. If anyone has no love for the Lord, let him be accursed. Our Lord, come! The grace of the Lord Jesus be with you. My love be with you all in Christ Jesus. Amen." (1 Corinthians 16:15-24)

The great hope of every Christian is the second coming of Jesus Christ. In chapter fifteen, Paul wrote about the promises of resurrected bodies and eternal life with the Lord. But until that day, we live in the tension of waiting. We struggle with sin, divisions, and trials, yet we also live with hope and assurance that Christ will return and fulfill every promise.

As Paul concludes this letter, he directs the Corinthians—and us— to live faithfully as we wait. His prayer, *"Our Lord, come!"* (v. 22), reflects the longing for Jesus to return and set all things right. Like Paul, Christians across generations have lived with the expectation of Christ's return, knowing each day brings us closer to that moment.

But how do we wait well? Paul offers practical and spiritual instructions:

1. **Devotion to Service:** Paul highlights the example of Stephanas and his household, who were devoted to serving the saints. As we wait, we are called to be devoted to God's work and the care of others.
2. **Submission to Leaders:** Paul encourages the Corinthians to honor and support their leaders and fellow laborers. A spirit of humility and cooperation strengthens the body of Christ.
3. **Rejoicing in Community:** Paul rejoices in the refreshment provided by fellow believers like Stephanas, Fortunatus, and Achaicus. Community is vital for encouragement and renewal as we wait.
4. **Grace and Love:** Paul's farewell words emphasize the need to live in grace and extend love to one another. Our actions and interactions should reflect the grace we have received from Christ.
5. **Hope in Christ's Return:** Paul anchors his closing in the ultimate hope of Christ's return. This hope gives purpose to our waiting and strength to endure trials.

Waiting is not passive; it's an active, faithful pursuit of God's will in our lives. We wait with hope, not despair, because Christ's return is certain. While we long for that day, we are called to live in His grace, serve His people, and proclaim His Gospel.

■ *Reflection:*

How are you embracing Paul's final instructions? Are you living in grace, serving faithfully, and setting your heart on the hope of Christ's return? What does God want you to know about waiting well?

■ *Prayer:*

Lord, thank You for the promise of Your return. Teach me to wait with hope and faithfulness. Help me to live in Your grace, to serve others with love, and to rejoice in the community You have given me. Come, Lord Jesus, come! Amen.

Epilogue: Are You Moving from Glory to Glory?

Scripture and Prayer:

"O God who before the passion of your only begotten Son revealed his glory upon the holy mountain: Grant to us that we, beholding by faith the light of his countenance, may be strengthened to bear our cross, and be changed into his likeness from glory to glory; through Jesus Christ our Lord, who lives and reigns with you and the Holy Spirit, one God, for ever and ever. Amen."

— Book of Common Prayer,
   The Collect for the Last Sunday after the Epiphany

As the season of Epiphany concludes, we are invited to enter the holy season of Lent, a time set apart for repentance, fasting, prayer, and transformation. Lent offers a sacred opportunity to reflect on Christ's journey to the cross and what it means for us to take up our own cross and follow Him.

But why observe Lent? Not to earn God's love—His love for you is already perfect and complete. Rather, Lent is a time to respond to that love, to grow in faith, and to align your life more closely with His will. The season calls us to step away from worldly distractions and comforts, to make room for the Spirit to work within us, and to be transformed into the likeness of Christ.

During Lent, we are invited to deny ourselves, not for the sake of self-punishment but for liberation. Self-denial—whether through fasting, giving up a comfort, or taking on a spiritual discipline— helps loosen the grip of worldly attachments on our hearts. It creates space for God's Word to take root in us, for His Spirit to convict and renew us, and for His glory to shine through us.

Jesus laid down His life for you, and Lent offers the chance to lay down something in return, be it a habit, an indulgence, or a distraction. At the same time, it is a season to take up practices that draw you closer to Him: Scripture reading, prayer, fasting, service, or acts of love and mercy. These disciplines help tune your heart to His, reminding you of His sacrifice and conforming you to His image.

As the Collect reminds us, beholding Christ's glory strengthens us to bear our cross and transforms us *"from glory to glory"* (2 Corinthians 3:18). Through this transformation, we are made more fully into the image of the one who created and redeemed us. Lent is not a season of shame but a season of grace, a time to grow into the fullness of who God has called you to be.

Even if you falter in your Lenten commitments, remember that His grace is sufficient. The goal is not perfection in practice but progress in faith and love.

■ *Reflection:*

How will you observe a holy Lent this year? What is God inviting you to lay down or take up for the next forty days? What steps can you take to draw closer to Him and allow His Spirit to transform you from glory to glory?

■ *Prayer:*

Lord, as I enter this season of Lent, help me to behold Your glory and be transformed by it. Strengthen me to bear my cross, to grow in grace, and to reflect Your love to the world. May this holy season bring me closer to You, changing me from glory to glory. Amen.

www.ingramcontent.com/pod-product-compliance
Lightning Source LLC
Chambersburg PA
CBHW061802070526
44586CB00023B/2685